'I Did It' Mathematics

Second Edition

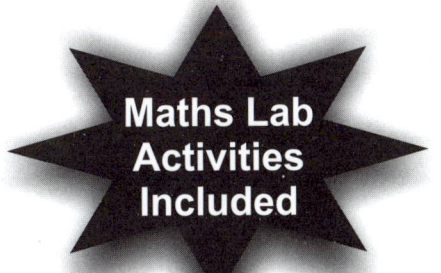

Sudha Mahesh

CAMBRIDGE UNIVERSITY PRESS

Cambridge, New York, Melbourne, Madrid, Cape Town, Singapore,
São Paulo, Delhi, Dubai, Tokyo

Cambridge University Press
4381/4 Ansari Road, Daryaganj, Delhi 110002, India

www.cambridge.org
Information on this title: www.cambridge.org/9780521185219

© Cambridge University Press 2011

This publication is in copyright. Subject to statutory exception
and to the provisions of relevant collective licensing agreements,
no reproduction of any part may take place without the written
permission of Cambridge University Press.

First published 2011

Printed in India at Sanat Printers, Kundli

A catalogue for this publication is available from the British Library

ISBN 978-0-521-18521-9 Paperback

Additional resources for this publication at www.cambridgeindia.org

Cambridge University Press has no responsibility for the persistence or
accuracy of URLs for external or third-party internet websites referred to in
this publication, and does not guarantee that any content on such websites is,
or will remain, accurate or appropriate.

Contents

	Overview	iv
	Preface	x
1.	Patterns	1
2.	Numbers	3
3.	Numbers in Operations	14
4.	Test of Divisibility	28
5.	Powers of Numbers	33
6.	H.C.F. and L.C.M.	38
7.	Fractions	47
8.	Decimals	58
9.	Percentage	74
10.	Ratio and Proportion	83
11.	Profit and Loss	89
12.	Simple Interest	94
13.	Unitary Method	101
14.	Bills	109
15.	Time	113
16.	Perimeter, Area and Volume	121
17.	Algebra	139
18.	Rotation, Reflection and Nets	144
19.	Angles	151
20.	Triangles	159
21.	Circles	166
22.	Graphs	174
23.	Money	180

Overview

Chapter	Chapter Name	Time Allotted	Content
1	Patterns	1 week	• Pattern making by using body parts • Patterns in numbers • Symmetrical patterns
2	Numbers	2 weeks	• Numbers up to 7 digits • Comparison of numbers up to 7 digits • Use of expanded form to write numbers • Numbers in Indian and International systems • Recognition of the number system of a number • Numbers in ascending and descending orders
3	Numbers in Operations	2 weeks	• Analyse problems to understand which operation should be applied • Terms related to all the four operations • Relationship between operations • Round numbers to the nearest 10, 100 and 1000 • Regroup numbers to perform the operations
4	Test of Divisibility	1 week	• Rules for division • Numbers to test the rules • Strategies to apply the skill learnt in day-to-day life
5	Powers of Numbers	1 week	• Exponential form in a given value • Changing numbers from exponential form to a whole number • Estimation of sums, products, differences and quotients for numbers that are in exponential form
6	H.C.F. and L.C.M.	2 weeks	• Definition of multiples and factors • Highest Common Factor (H.C.F.) and Least Common Multiple (L.C.M.) for two or more numbers • Different methods for finding H.C.F. and L.C.M.
7	Fractions	2 weeks	• Revision of proper, improper and mixed fractions • Ascending and descending order of fractions • Addition and subtraction of mixed numbers by regrouping as improper fractions • Multiplication and division of fractions • Estimation of sums, products and quotients of fractions
8	Decimals	3 weeks	• The four operations with decimals • Conversion of fractions into decimals and vice versa • Like and unlike decimals

Overview

Objective	Outcome
• To enhance the creativity of students by encouraging them to make their own patterns • To help them translate the patterns into body movements, which will help them understand the rhythm involved in it	The students will understand that they are surrounded by patterns, be it in nature, numbers, music or language.
• To recognise and read numbers in Indian and International systems • To read the same number in both the systems, grouping them differently each time • To understand how to use zero as a place holder, where necessary • To use big numbers in real-life situations	The students will understand place value of numbers up to 8 digits, both in Indian and International systems. They will also be able to use them in real-life situations.
• To understand the reasons of using an operation • To select appropriate methods for solving problems • To understand connections between different operations	The students will be able to use the appropriate operation, at the appropriate place. They will be able to analyse problems by identifying relationships. They will also be able to communicate their understanding while applying the concepts in their day-to-day life.
• To find out if a given number is divisible by a number at a glance, by applying the learnt rules • To do quick calculations	The students will be able to understand the usefulness of learning the tests of divisibility in their day-to-day life.
• To write numbers in short form • To find the total value, when given in exponential form	The students will be able to understand that a value can be expressed as a whole number or in exponential form. Knowing cube numbers and square numbers will help them while calculating area and volume in Geometry.
• To review Highest Common Factor and Least Common Multiple • To learn to decide whether a number is divisible by another or not • To use the knowledge of multiplication to find common multiples • To create and solve problems involving H.C.F. and L.C.M.	The students will be able to understand that the basic arithmetic operations, such as multiplication and division, are interconnected. They will also be able to identify patterns in numbers, as they work with factors and multiples.
• To understand that fractions can be multiplied and divided • To look at fractional parts of things in their immediate environment • To learn to convert mixed numbers into improper fractions and vice versa • To convert and order fractions	The students will understand different ways of looking at portions of a whole. Learning the concept helps them to distribute things in a group equitably in real-life situations. They will also learn to add up portions to make whole lots.
• To understand the relationship between fractions and decimals • To perform the four operations of arithmetic by using numbers with the decimal place • To compare decimal numbers up to thousandth place • To give the place value of a digit in a decimal number	The students will be able to use fractions and decimals in real-life situations. They will be able to rename decimals as fractions.

Chapter	Chapter Name	Time Allotted	Content
9	Percentage	2 weeks	• Definition of percentage • Conversion of fractions and decimals into per cent and vice versa • Per cent of a given number • Comparison of ratio, per cent, fraction and decimal
10	Ratio and Proportion	2 weeks	• Ratio as comparison of two or more things • Missing term in a proportion • Conversion of ratio to fraction • Ratio in its lowest term
11	Profit and Loss	1 week	• Definitions of cost price, selling price, profit and loss • Rules pertaining to profit and loss • Loss or profit percentage
12	Simple Interest	2 weeks	• Definition of 'simple interest' • Money and its purpose • Per cent of a number and applying this when the rate is given • Calculating percentage • Conversion of fractions into per cent
13	Unitary Method	1 week	• Definitions of 'direct variation' and 'inverse proportion' • Problems related to direct variation and inverse proportion
14	Bills	1 week	• Objectives of bills • Advantages of bills • Identifying the vital elements for making a bill
15	Time	2 week	• Reading a clock to the minute • Occurrence of seasons • Analogue clock versus digital clock • Time as a.m. and p.m. • Time as AD and BC
16	Perimeter, Area and Volume	3 weeks	• Description of area and perimeter • Area and perimeter of irregular shapes • Area and perimeter of polygons • Difference between area and perimeter • Concept of volume • Volume of cubes and cuboids

Objective	Outcome
- To understand, how to find percentage of a given number - To convert fractions and decimals into per cent and vice versa - To apply the concept to solve real-life situations - To find the percentage - To find the number when percentage is given	The students will be able to find percentages. They will also be able to apply the concept to evaluate their own performance in a classroom.
- To learn what ratio means and how to compare two things using a ratio - To learn to convert two or more quantities to the same unit - To reduce a ratio to its lowest term - To learn proportionality and apply it in real-life situations	The students will be able to compare and solve problems that involve ratio and proportion in real-life situations.
- To understand the meaning of profit and loss - To interpret the given data and solve problems to find profit or loss - To select the appropriate strategies for solving money problems - To explain the kind of decision they can take to solve problems	The students will be able to see the relationship between cost price and selling price and decide whether there is loss or profit. They will also be able to convert the loss or profit to percentage. They will be able to apply the concept in real-life situations while doing money transactions.
- To understand the meaning of simple interest - To describe and understand the usage of per cent in one's day-to-day life - To understand an increase or decrease in per cent, while creating and solving problems using simple interest	The students will be able to apply the concept in their real life, while calculating amounts. They will be able to convert fractions and decimals into per cent.
- To understand the meaning and application of the two concepts - To make inferences on the basis of the available data - To evaluate the formulae when the replacements for the variables are given - To express their comparisons using the symbols	The students will be able to differentiate between direct variation and inverse proportion. They will be able to use their understanding in their day-to-day dealings and make convincing arguments.
- To connect operations learnt with application in day-to-day life - To learn about bills - To learn to plan expenditure against funds - To learn to use money and to know how measures are used in trade	The students will learn how to check the list and what all to look for while shopping. It will help to make them aware of different prices prevalent in the market and thus plan their expenditure accordingly.
- To understand the difference between an analog clock and a digital clock - To convert time from an analog into digital clock	The students will understand time to the minute and value it. They will be able to read and interpret time in a 12 as well as 24 hour clock.
- To learn the difference between area and perimeter - To demonstrate the relationship between area and perimeter - To use the formulae to find area and perimeter - To determine the volume of objects by using the formulae	The students will understand the difference between perimeter, area and volume. They will have good spatial understanding. The students will also learn to solve problems in their immediate environment. They would understand that with the same perimeter, we can have different areas.

Chapter	Chapter Name	Time Allotted	Content
17	Algebra	2 weeks	• Algebra as a branch of Mathematics • Variables and constants • Terms related to Algebra
18	Rotation, Reflection and Nets	1 week	• Definitions of rotation and reflection • Transformation of a figure without changing its size or shape • Turning a figure around a point
19	Angles	1 week	• Different types of angles based on their measurement • Definitions for different types of angles • Estimating, describing and constructing angles • Definition and ways of using a protractor
20	Triangles	2 weeks	• Definition of triangles • Attributes of triangles • Three angles of triangles • Measurements of the third angle, when the other two angles are given
21	Circles	2 weeks	• Properties of circles • Differences between a circle and other plane shapes • Radius and the diameter of a circle • Definitions for various parts of a circle • Construction of a circle with a pair of compass and naming the parts • Circumference of a circle
22	Graphs	1 week	• Types of graphs • Steps to follow while making a graph
23	Money	2 weeks	• Operations involving money – multiplication and division. • Problem solving using money

Objective	Outcome
<ul><li>To understand Algebra as a branch of Mathematics</li><li>To use a variable as a place holder</li><li>To understand the concept of variables and expressions</li><li>To differentiate and express different expressions as monomial, binomial and polynomial</li><li>To use variables, expressions and unequal groups for solving problems</li></ul>	The students will be able to understand the difference between a variable and a constant. They will understand that a letter can be used as a place holder to substitute numbers. They will be able to create number patterns using constants and variables.
<ul><li>To know the meaning of rotation</li><li>To understand every rotation has a centre</li><li>To understand that reflection means producing the mirror image of an object</li></ul>	The students will understand the difference between rotation and reflection. They will be able to create several attractive patterns by rotating figures as well as by reflecting figures.
<ul><li>To learn to identify angles as acute, right, obtuse, straight and reflex</li><li>To learn to estimate and measure angles using a protractor</li><li>To construct different angles using the available information</li><li>To apply spatial reasoning while constructing angles</li></ul>	The students will be able to construct different angles using the protractor. It will improve the spatial understanding of the students. It will also help them understand directions and make inferences based on the available information, while dealing with real-life situations.
<ul><li>To recognise different types of triangles</li><li>To understand the attributes of triangles</li><li>To learn to use a protractor for measuring angles</li><li>To visualise and communicate understanding of triangles with the help of models</li></ul>	The students will learn that unlike many other plane figures, a triangle can be of various types. They will learn the different attributes of triangles and, through their own creative thinking, will be able to develop an understanding of the solution, i.e., 'The sum of the three angles of any triangle = $180°$'.
<ul><li>To differentiate between circle and other shapes by looking at its parts</li><li>To construct circles with different radii</li><li>To draw and name the parts of a circle</li><li>To identify and compare circles with other shapes</li><li>To learn to define all the parts of a circle</li></ul>	The students will be able to understand and appreciate a circle as a different kind of plane shape. They will be able to identify and understand its geometric properties. They will also learn the appropriate vocabulary to describe each part and solve questions using their spatial understanding.
<ul><li>To gather information and interpret the same using a graph</li><li>To interpret a graph</li><li>To infer a large amount of information quickly and easily</li></ul>	The students will be able to collect, interpret and present statistics easily and quickly through graphs. They will also learn to understand the kind of information one needs to construct graphs.
<ul><li>To learn to multiply and divide money in real-life situations</li><li>To learn to separate rupees and paise by a decimal point</li><li>To learn to value money</li><li>To handle money properly and accurately</li></ul>	The students will understand the importance of earning, saving and spending money, and its wise usage.

Preface to the first edition

'I Did It' Mathematics encourages students to understand the interrelationship between different topics. It initiates students into the process of learning by discovery and helps develop confidence to work individually as well as in groups. The tasks and activities in the book provide them with ample opportunity to think and actively participate in learning new concepts. It also aims to integrate mathematical concepts with other subjects.

The book promotes mathematical thinking and provides comprehensive lesson plans, designed to assess and reinforce learning. In-text activities have been included to develop skills for applying mathematics in day-to-day life. There are tips for teaching and enrichment activities in every unit. Initial activities in the chapters are focussed on whole class participation.

Sticker sheets are available for fun and development of efficient motor skills.

Preface to the second edition

'I Did It' Mathematics is a nine-level series of textbooks in mathematics that has been prepared in conformity with the latest NCERT syllabus and the National Curriculum Framework (2005). The thoroughly revised edition of the series *'I Did It' Mathematics* has been redesigned to make the learning of mathematical concepts an active process, which is an important curriculum need. It provides plenty of opportunities to 'Do and discover' through individual and co-operative work and at the same time paves the path for advanced learning through simple explanations and information.

Mathematics is about a certain way of thinking and reasoning. The students need to understand the logic behind the mathematical concepts. The series best achieves this by building on activities and exercises that help the learner establish an association of the concept with real life. *Maths Lab Activities*, incorporated in each chapter, tune the learner's thinking pattern to the ensuing lesson. This helps to grasp the basic principles in a fun way and also reinforces learning. Word problems under *Word Attack* train the students to apply the concepts learnt to problem solving in their day-to-day life.

An *Overview* at the beginning of each book sets clear guidelines for the teachers with respect to weightage and time to be allotted per topic, the objectives and outcomes.

The series builds on the mathematical skills with a perfect balance between fun, and drill and skill.

Sudha Mahesh

Chapter 1

Patterns

You know...
- patterns are found everywhere in the environment
- patterns are infinite and repeat themselves over and over again
- there are patterns in nature, music, art, language and Mathematics
- patterns can be circular or linear
- patterns can be natural or man-made.

Maths Lab Activity 1

Material required

Cards having patterns drawn on them, as shown below

Method (Note for the Teacher)

Divide the class into groups. Give each group a card with a pattern drawn on it. The pattern should be formed by lines, as shown below. The students should decide how to demonstrate that pattern by using their body parts. They can clap hands, tap feet, nod heads or sway their bodies.

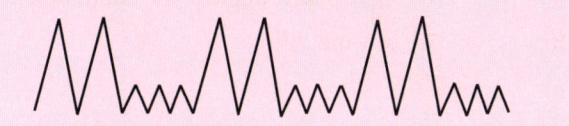 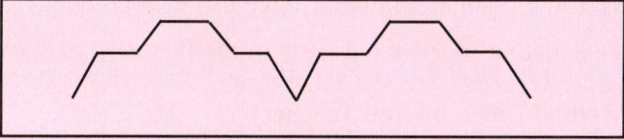

Exercise 1

Now draw any two pictures that show circular and linear patterns.

Exercise 2

You know numbers can also form patterns.

Given below are some numerical patterns. Look at each one of them carefully and write a line to say what pattern is followed by each.

(a) 120, 125, 130, 135, 140, ...   The pattern here is counting by 5.

(b) 1, 2, 4, 8, 16, 32, ...   _____

(c) 5, 10, 20, 40, 80, ...   _____

(d) 90, 81, 73, 66, 60, 55, ...   _____

(e) 100, 110, 90, 100, 80, 90, ...   _____

Symmetrical Patterns

Symmetry means having the same pattern on both sides laterally, or on top and bottom. You must have seen the wings of butterflies. They have symmetrical patterns on both the wings.

Maths Lab Activity 2

Material required

(a) Liquid paints, in two or three different colours
(b) One paper napkin for each student
(c) A cutout of the main body of the butterfly, as shown below
(d) An ink filler

Method (Note for the Teacher)

Ask the students to fold the paper napkin into four equal parts. Ask them to put a few drops of each colour on the paper napkin by using the ink filler. The paint will smudge and spread. When they will unfold the paper napkin, they will see a beautiful symmetrical pattern. They can cut it into the shape of the wings of a butterfly. Ask them to stick the cutout of the pattern on either side of the butterfly, as shown below. They will have a pretty butterfly.

(The cutout should be big enough to accomodate the wings made.)

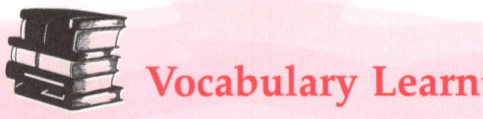

Vocabulary Learnt

natural   repeat   circular

man-made   linear

infinite

Chapter 2

Numbers

You know...

- numbers can be grouped according to the Hindu Arabic or International System
- numbers up to eight digits
- how to arrange numbers in ascending and descending order
- how to write number names for numbers up to eight digits.

Maths Lab Activity 1

Materials required

1 to 100 number cards

Method (Note for the Teacher)

Revise different kinds of numbers like odd, even, prime and composite with the students. Tell them that you will be showing cards at random and they have to say what kind of number each is. Some cards may have two attributes. For examples, 5 is both an odd and a prime number. Accept both the answers in such a case.

Decimal System

You must have noticed that we follow the decimal system in our day-to-day life. The decimal system is also known as the base-10 system. Each place value towards the left becomes ten times more than the previous one. In fact, 'deci' means 10. Therefore, it is called the decimal system. Only ten different numerals are used to represent all the decimal numbers. These are 0 to 9.

Ten thousands	Thousands	Hundreds	Tens	Ones	Tenths	Hundredths	Thousandths

10 times more ← Start → 10 times less

Binary System

Base-2 number system is used in computers for all its calculations. Unlike base-10, base-2 has no name for its place value. Each place is two times more than the previous place on its right. Hence, it is called the binary system, where 'bi' means 2.

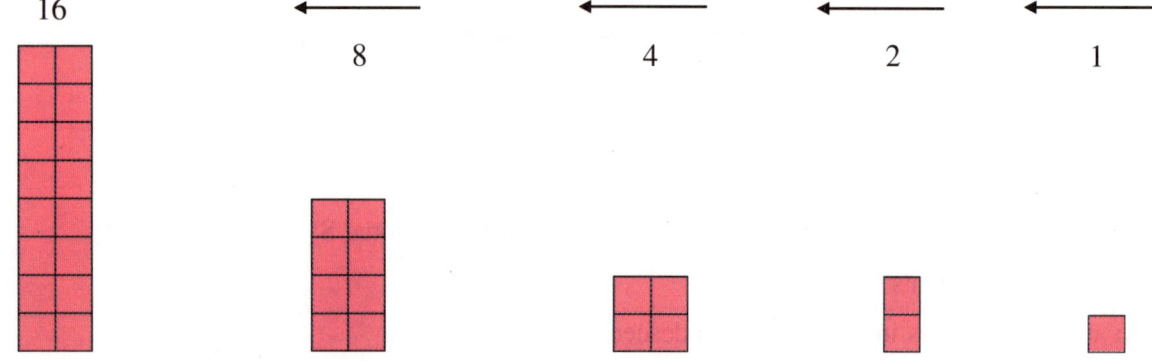

Now, learn to write the numbers 1 to 10 in base-10.

Decimal system	Binary system	
1	1	
2	10	(Since the single ☐ is not needed, you write 0 in its place and 1 next to it, as you are taking a ▭.)
3	11	(a single ☐ and a double ▭)
4	100	(Just take ⊞ and fill the other two places with zeroes.)
5	101	(☐ and ⊞. So ▭ place is filled with 0.)

Now, change the following base-10 numbers to base-2 numbers. Use diagrams. If any place value is not used, put a zero there.

Example   Base-10   Drawing in base-2   Number in base-2

3   ▭ ☐   1 1

Exercise 1

Complete the table.

Number in base-10	Drawings for the number in base-2	Number in base-2
6		
10		
7		
9		
8		

Exercise 2

Change to base-10.

Base-2	Base-10
10	2
1010	
111	
1000	
10100	
100	

Numbers can also be written by using two different systems – the Hindu Arabic System and the International System. To which system a given number belongs, can be found out from the way it is separated into periods by using a comma and from the name given to each place after ten thousand.

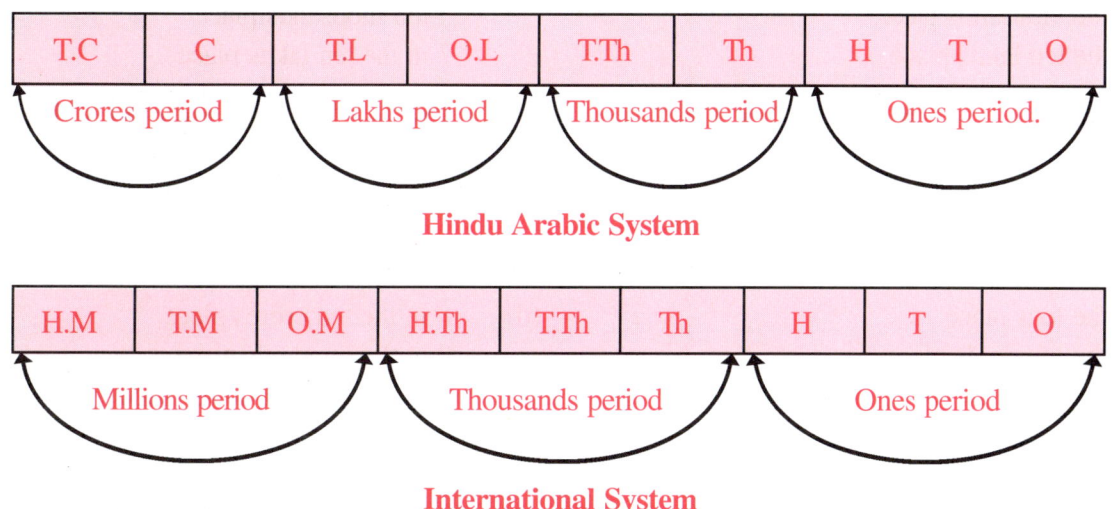

Hindu Arabic System

International System

Look at this number.

4 2 7 0 8 5 3 9 1

Separate the number into periods according to the Indian system by using commas. Next, write its number name.

_____

_____

Now, separate the number into periods according to the International system by using commas. Next, write its number name.

_____

_____

Exercise 3

Arrange the following numbers under their correct place value and put the commas at the right places. Remember to use zero as a 'place holder', wherever necessary.

Example

    3 in the hundreds place
    7 in the ten lakhs place
    6 in the ones place
    5 in the one crores place
    8 in the ten thousands place

O.C	T.L	O.L	T.Th	O.Th	H	T	O
5,	7	0,	8	0,	3	0	6

Now, complete the following.

(a)   9 in the ten thousands place
      7 in the one crores place
      4 in the ones place
      2 in the thousands place
      5 in the ten lakhs place

T.C	O.C	T.L	O.L	T.Th	O.Th	H	T	O

(b)   9 in the one lakhs place
      0 in the ones place
      6 in the ten crores place
      5 ten thousands place
      7 in the ten lakhs place

T.C	O.C	T.L	O.L	T.Th	O.Th	H	T	O

(c)   9 in the tens place
      2 in the hundreds place
      6 in the one lakhs place
      3 in the thousands place
      4 in the ten thousands place

T.C	O.C	T.L	O.L	T.Th	O.Th	H	T	O

(d)   8 in the ten crores place
      0 in the hundreds place
      7 in the ten thousands place
      5 in the one crores place
      6 in the tens place

T.C	O.C	T.L	O.L	T.Th	O.Th	H	T	O

(e)   3 in the thousands place
      6 in the hundreds place
      2 in the ten crores place
      5 in the ones place
      8 in ten lakhs place

T.C	O.C	T.L	O.L	T.Th	O.Th	H	T	O

(f)   1 in the hundred thousands place
      2 in the hundreds place
      6 in the thousands place
      9 in the one millions place
      0 in the ones place

H.M	T.M	O.M	H.Th	T.Th	O.Th	H	T	O

(g) 5 in the ten millions place
0 in the ones place
1 in the ten thousands place
7 in the hundreds place
2 in the hundred thousands place

H.M	T.M	O.M	H.Th	T.Th	O.Th	H	T	O

(h) 9 in the hundred millions place
3 in the ones place
2 in the ten thousands place
0 in the hundred thousands place
6 in the hundreds place

H.M	T.M	O.M	H.Th	T.Th	O.Th	H	T	O

(i) 0 in the one thousands place
5 in ten thousands place
2 in the one millions place
1 in the hundred millions place
9 in the tens place

H.M	T.M	O.M	H.Th	T.Th	O.Th	H	T	O

(j) 7 in the ones place
0 in the hundreds place
7 in the hundred thousands place
7 in the tens place
7 in the ten millions place

H.M	T.M	O.M	H.Th	T.Th	O.Th	H	T	O

Exercise 4

Write the standard numeral and its number name in the Hindu Arabic System.

2000000 400000 3000 100 10 8	=	24,03,118 Twenty four lakhs, three thousand, one hundred and eighteen
(a) 6000000 500000 30000 800 10	=	

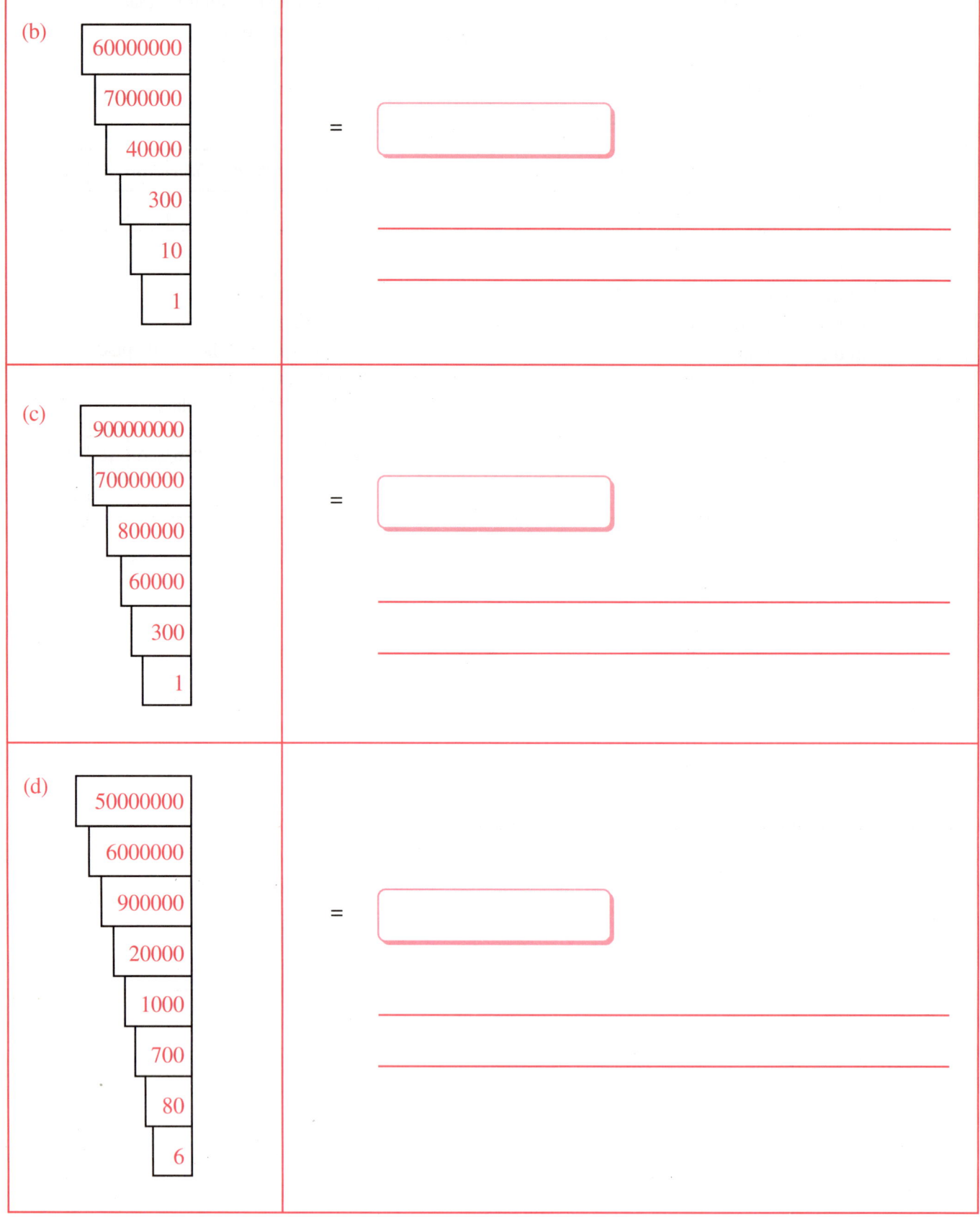

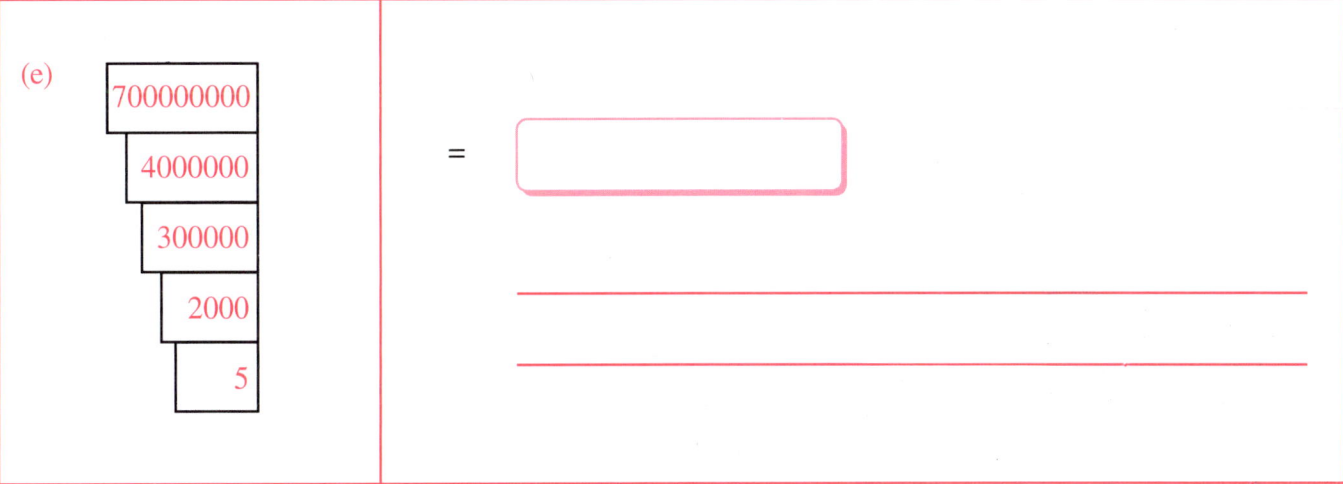

Exercise 5

Write in expanded form.

Example   56,89,357 = 5000000 + 600000 + 80000 + 9000 + 300 + 50 + 7

(a) 7,63,89,412 _____

(b) 49,85,162 _____

(c) 5,00,78,916 _____

(d) 8,41,23,756 _____

(e) 76,54,321 _____

(f) 83,14,790 _____

(g) 6,04,01,020 _____

(h) 93,12,756 _____

(i) 80,00,491 _____

(j) 6,43,85,712 _____

Exercise 6

Read carefully and find out the system to which the number belongs.

Next, write the standard numeral using place value and commas at the correct places.

Example

4 ten thousands
8 hundreds
7 thousands
9 ones
7 lakhs

Look for the highest place value and write down all the place values to the right of it. Then write the numbers.

Hindu Arabic

L	T.Th	Th	H	T	O
7,	4	7,	8	0	9

		Number system	Standard number
(a)	6 thousands 9 ones 7 ten thousands 8 hundreds 7 tens		
(b)	4 ten lakhs 7 ten thousands 6 tens 5 ones 8 hundreds		
(c)	5 thousands 7 ones 2 millions 8 hundreds 7 ten thousands		
(d)	3 tens 6 ten thousands 2 ones 7 ten millions 5 thousands		

Exercise 7

Write number names for the following, both in the Hindu Arabic System and the International System, in your notebook.

(a) 783108494 (b) 913049167 (c) 217,894,729 (d) 410037512 (e) 258,420,301

Exercise 8

Match the following.

(a)	1000		the greatest 4-digit number
(b)	11		one less than the smallest 2-digit number
(c)	99		the smallest 6-digit number
(d)	9		the greatest 2-digit number
(e)	100000		one more than the smallest 2-digit number
(f)	9999		the smallest 4-digit number

Exercise 9

Use all the seven digits to write four different numbers of your choice.

(a) 4, 7, 9, 3, 0, 2, 1

| | | | |

(b) 7, 0, 3, 9, 1, 1, 0

| | | | |

(c) 5, 2, 0, 7, 8, 3, 1

| | | | |

(d) 5, 0, 8, 1, 2, 8, 7

| | | | |

(e) 9, 0, 0, 4, 2, 1, 3

| | | | |

(f) 6, 8, 4, 6, 9, 2, 1

| | | | |

Making 100

Here is an interesting activity that helps you get 100 each time you follow the instructions clearly.

Follow the steps.

(a) Think of a number less than 10. For example, 3.
(b) Double that number. 3 + 3 = 6.
(c) Add the number that you thought of to this answer. 6 + 3 = 9.
(d) Multiply the answer by 2. 9 × 2 = 18.
(e) Subtract the number you thought of from the answer. 18 – 3 = 15.
(f) Divide the answer by the number you thought of. 15 divided by 3 = 5.
(g) Multiply the answer by 10. 5 × 10 = 50.
(h) Double the answer. 50 + 50 = 100.

Now take another number less than 100. Follow the same steps and see if you can get hundred.

Vocabulary Learnt

standard numeral   expanded   binary

period   decimal

base   calculations   place holder

Maths Lab Activity 2

Materials required

(a) 1 to 100 number grid for each group
(b) Worksheet with just the arrows, as shown in Sheet 1
(c) Worksheet with the starting number and the last number, as shown in Sheet 2

Method (Note for the Teacher)

Divide the students into groups. Give to each group a number grid and the two worksheets. Ask the students to find out the number they will reach each time by following the steps indicated by the arrows. (Each arrow indicates one step.)

Ask them to draw arrows to reach the last number as in Sheet 2.

1 to 100 Number Grid

1	2	3	4	5	6	7	8	9	10
11	12	13	14	15	16	17	18	19	20
21	22	23	24	25	26	27	28	29	30
31	32	33	34	35	36	37	38	39	40
41	42	43	44	45	46	47	48	49	50
51	52	53	54	55	56	57	58	59	60
61	62	63	64	65	66	67	68	69	70
71	72	73	74	75	76	77	78	79	80
81	82	83	84	85	86	87	88	89	90
91	92	93	94	95	96	97	98	99	100

When you go one step up from a number, you reach 10 numbers less than the previous number. In the same way, when you go one step down from a number, you reach 10 numbers more than the previous number.

When you move one step to the right you reach one number more. In the same way, if you move one step to the left, you reach a number less.

Sheet 1

(a) 56 → → ↑↑↑ → = ☐

(b) 78 ↑↑↑↑ ← ← = ☐

(c) 34 ↓↓↓ → → ↑ = ☐

(d) 12 ↑ ← ↓↓↓↓ = ☐

Sheet 2

(a) 34 [___] = 67

(b) 56 [___] = 81

(c) 23 [___] = 49

(d) 98 [___] = 35

Chapter 3 — Numbers in Operations

You know...
- Arithmetic has four operations
- addition and multiplication belong to one family of facts
- subtraction and division belong to one family of facts
- how to apply the operations in real-life situations.

Maths Lab Activity 1

Materials required

(a) Blackboard   (b) Chalk   (c) Paper   (d) Pencil

Method (Note for the Teacher)

Divide the students into groups. Write a 4- or 5-digit number on the blackboard. Tell the students to write a sentence each showing the four operations for that number.

For example, if you give the number 1250, students can write

$1000 + 250 = 1250$, $2000 - 750 = 1250$, $5 \times 250 = 1250$ and $1250 \div 25 = 50$.

Choose the numbers carefully beforehand. Do not use prime numbers or difficult numbers. This is just to revise the four operations before beginning the chapter.

Arithmetic has four operations.

| Addition | Subtraction | Multiplication | Division |

Addition

(a) Addition involves combining numbers together.

(b) The numbers that are added are called 'addends' and the answer obtained is called the 'sum'.

(c) Addition of numbers can be done with and without renaming.

(d) Adding the addends, in any order, does not alter the sum.

(e) The process of adding larger numbers is the same as that of adding smaller numbers.

(f) Addition has similar properties like multiplication.

(g) Multiplication is repeated addition of the same number.

Example 1

650970431 + 800926415

	H.M	T.M	O.M	H.Th	T.Th	O.Th	H	T	O
	6	5	0	9	7	0	4	3	1
+	8	0	0	9	2	6	4	1	5
1	4	5	1	8	9	6	8	4	6

> **Remember!**
> Write the greatest number first, then the second greatest, third greatest and so on.

Example 2

13654617 + 205891 + 522 + 31

	C	T.Th	L	T.Th	Th	H	T	O
	1	3	6	5	4	6	1	7
			2	0	5	8	9	1
					5	2	2	
+							3	1
	1	3	8	6	1	0	6	1

> **Remember!**
> Every number must have the ones place.

> **Remember!**
> If you add any number with 0, you will get the same number as the answer.

Exercise 1

Add the following.

(a) 60237141 + 29710353

(b) 62158211 + 21150863

(c) 2585231 + 6251432

(d) 25135151 + 11621813

(e) 198176 + 986683

(f) 5632156 + 6321515

(g) 987116281 + 256315211

(h) 100852315 + 20505819

(i) 9650833313 + 3330569

Exercise 2

Add the following.

(a) 40 + 654321 + 5 + 489 + 500631

(b) 608 + 51239651 + 3232 + 99 + 1

(c) 998768599 + 1101 + 11 + 1 + 10000102

(d) 66 + 598 + 956201 + 8450633 + 121212121

(e) 11111 + 1010101 + 110110110 + 1 + 999

(f) 79654328 + 582 + 5 + 6362 + 60

(g) 616543 + 9 + 912 + 918918 + 632182516

(h) 9872 + 98 + 7 + 9898 + 53 + 62150404

Subtraction

(a) Subtraction is taking away a number from another larger number.
(b) The number to be subtracted is called the 'subtrahend'.
(c) The number you subtract from is called the 'minuend'.
(d) Division is repeated subtraction of the same number.

Look at these examples.

Example 1 Here, you have to borrow and rename since the subtrahend is greater than the minuend.

	C	T.Th	L	T.Th.	Th	H	T	O
	9	8	4	5	2	7	8	4
−	6	1	2	1	1	4	4	5
	3	7	2	4	1	3	3	9

Example 2 Subtract 83261075 and 65841719.

	C	T.Th	L	T.Th.	Th	H	T	O
	8	3	2	6	1	0	7	5
−	6	5	8	4	1	7	1	9
	1	7	4	1	9	3	5	6

Exercise 3

Subtract the following.

(a) 3 9 4 5 9 8 7
 − 2 6 3 1 7 9 8
 ─────────────

(b) 8 7 9 9 6 2 5
 − 6 4 7 7 7 8 4
 ─────────────

(c) 5 8 9 6 1 2 2 3
 − 3 0 2 7 5 7 8 1
 ─────────────

(d) 1 0 0 0 0 0
 − 2 3 6 1 5
 ─────────────

(e) 9 8 1 1 5 3 4 1 3
 − 1 1 2 2 9 7 1 0 9
 ─────────────

(f) 2 5 4 3 1 7
 − 2 4 3 1 9
 ─────────────

Sometimes, you may have to fill in the missing digits of the subtrahend or the minuend.

Example

	T.L	L	T.Th	Th	H	T	O
	6	3	5	1	◯	4	◯
−	◯	4	1	◯	0	2	2
	3	9	3	3	7	2	1

Here,

Step 1: 3 – 2 = 1   Step 2: 4 – 2 = 2
Step 3: 7 – 0 = 7   Step 4: 11 – 8 = 3
Step 5: 4 – 1 = 3   Step 6: 13 – 4 = 9
Step 7: 5 – 2 = 3

	T.L	L	T.Th	Th	H	T	O
	6	3	5	1	7	4	3
–	2	4	1	8	0	2	2
	3	9	3	3	7	2	1

Exercise 4

Solve the following.

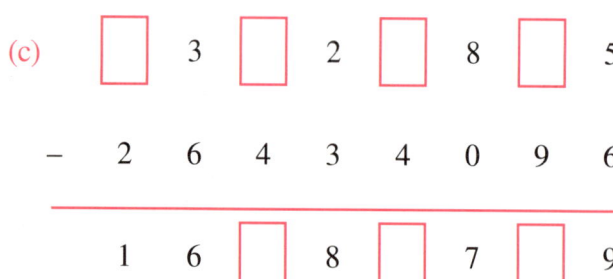

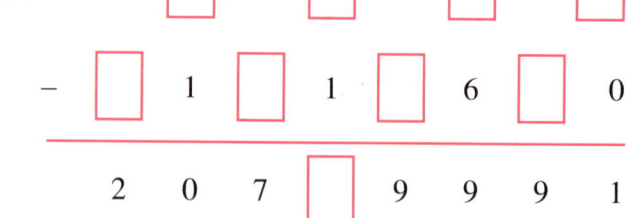

Multiplication

(a) Multiplication is repeated addition of the same number.

(b) It is a quick way of adding the same number repeatedly.

(c) Multiplying a number by zero gives zero as the answer.

(d) Multiplying a number by one gives the same number as answer.

(e) Multiplication has the same properties as addition.

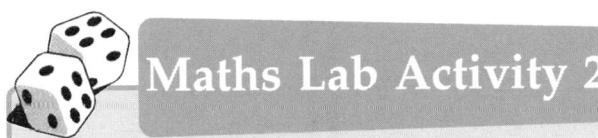 **Maths Lab Activity 2**

Materials required

The multiplication song

Method (Note for the Teacher)

Songs are not only interesting to learn but also a quick way of teaching concepts. Set the song given below to any favourite tune and teach the students.

Arithmetic has four operations,
That are used by all generations.
Multiplication is one of the games,
By you or me, it's played the same.

To multiply, you need at least two numbers,
Nothing can be done without these members.
'Times' is a very very special word,
Its multiplication when it is heard.

The number you start with is multiplicand,
The number that follows is multiplier.
The answer – Oh! Don't you know
Is the product, the product, the product.

Multiplication is nothing but a collection
Of equal groups for perfection.
It is commutative, associative, distributive,
You'll learn these when you are attentive.

When you want to increase something a number of times,
Multiplication gets you ahead – in the line.
It's a quick way to add equal groups
That follow one another like army troops.

With multiplication, you can't fail
We all know very well it's not vague.
Four times five is always a score,
And two times two is definitely four.

'Multiplication' – saves time and trouble,
If you don't know it, it's just terrible.
The only way to learn it is by rote
I didn't know it, so I wrote and wrote.

Example   Multiply 86453 by 5524.

				T.Th	Th	H	T	O	
				8	6	4	5	3	
			×		6	5	2	4	
				3	4	5	8	1	2	(86453 × 4)
			1	7	2	9	0	6	0	(86453 × 20)
		4	3	2	2	6	5	0	0	(86453 × 500)
	5	1	8	7	1	8	0	0	0	(86453 × 6000)
	5	6	4	0	1	9	3	7	2	

Exercise 5

Multiply.

(a) 25431 × 624   (b) 54360 × 618   (c) 82937 × 496   (d) 71098 × 1234

(e) 15863 × 2373   (f) 94467 × 5793   (g) 65812 × 4121   (h) 91819 × 9191

(i) 62493 × 9876   (j) 563412 × 789   (k) 41275 × 302   (l) 31476 × 1438

Patterns in Multiplication

We see patterns in multiplication. Some patterns are given below.

```
            1       ×       1         =           1
          1   1     ×     1   1       =         1 2 1
        1   1   1   ×   1   1   1     =       1 2 3 2 1
      1   1   1   1 × 1   1   1   1   =     1 2 3 4 3 2 1
```

Complete the pattern.

(a) 9 × 9 − 2 × 2 = 81 − 4 = 77
     89 × 89 − 12 × 12 = 7921 − 144 = 7777

888889 × 888889 − 111112 × 111112 = _____

Complete the next 4 steps in the pattern.

(b) 7 × 7 − 4 × 4 = 33
     67 × 67 − 34 × 34 = 3333
     667 × 667 − 334 × 334 = 333333

Division

(a) Division is the process of finding out how many times one number will 'fit into' the given number.
(b) Division does not have as many properties as addition or multiplication.
(c) Division is repeated subtraction of the same number.
(d) Rounding the divisor helps in doing calculations quickly.

Rounding Numbers

For the sake of convenience, we often round numbers to the nearest multiples of 10, 100, 1000 and so on. However, this gives only the approximate value.

Here are some questions for which approximate answers would do.

(a) How many people live in your village?   Around 5000
(b) How far is the station from your house?   Around 25 km
(c) What do you think is the weight of that lady? Around 100 kg
(d) How many students are there in your school? Around 500 students

These are questions that do not require specific answers. So they can be answered this way.

But how does one decide to which number the given number should be rounded?

Look at this.

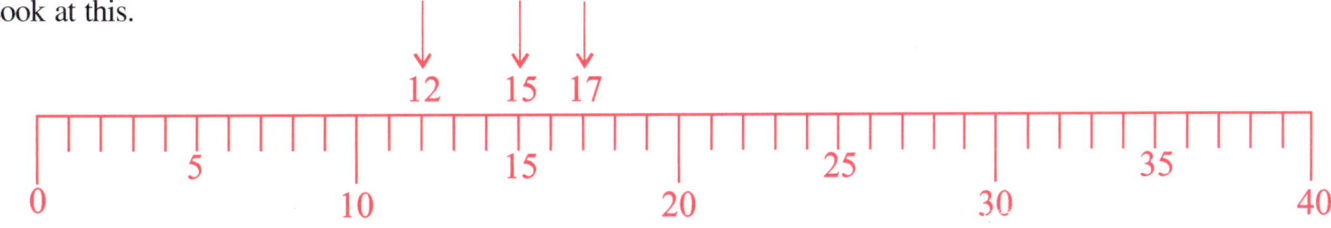

This number line is divided into tens.

If you look at 12, it is closer to 10 than to 20, which is the next tens number. So you round it to 10. If you take 17, it is closer to 20 than to 10. So, you round it to 20. If you take 15, it is midway between 10 and 20. In such a case, you should always round it to the ten that comes to the right, i.e., the one which is greater than the number.

Now look at this number line.

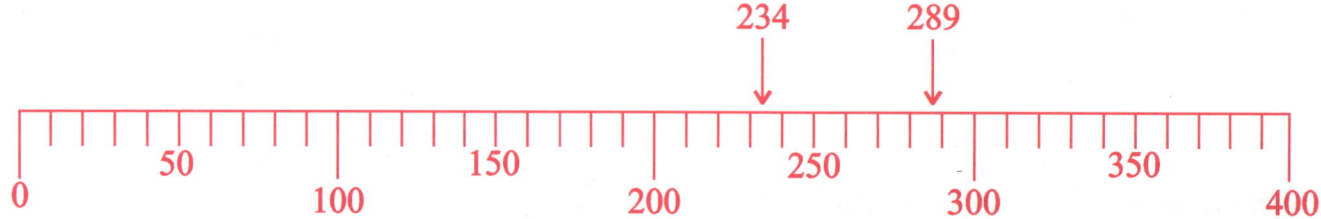

If you look at a number like 234, it comes before 250, which is midway between 200 and 300. So it should be rounded to 200, which is closer. A number like 250 should be rounded to 300. Also, a number like 289 should be rounded to 300 because it comes after 250 and is closer to 300.

Look at this number line.

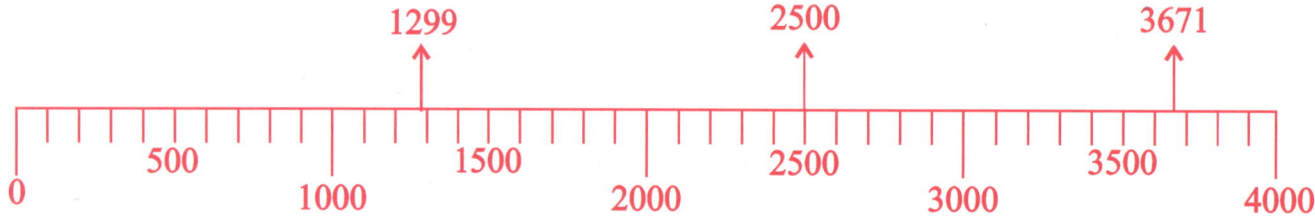

A number like 1299 should be rounded to 1000, a number like 2500 should be rounded to 3000. A number like 3671 should be rounded to 4000.

Exercise 6

(a) Round to the nearest 10.

(i) 45 ☐   (ii) 67 ☐   (iii) 34 ☐

(iv) 89 ☐   (v) 29 ☐   (vi) 65 ☐

(b) Round to the nearest 100.

(i) 234 ☐   (ii) 675 ☐   (iii) 921 ☐

(iv) 536 ☐   (v) 789 ☐   (vi) 235 ☐

(c) Round to the nearest 1000.

(i) 3452 ☐   (ii) 4589 ☐   (iii) 1234 ☐

(iv) 8907 ☐   (v) 5649 ☐   (vi) 4360 ☐

Rounding numbers is very useful in division. Dividing by big numbers is difficult as it is not possible to memorise the multiplication tables of every number. In such a case, rounding the divisor to multiples of 10, 100 or 1000 makes the calculations easier.

Example

Divide 4325 by 123. 123 can be rounded to 100.

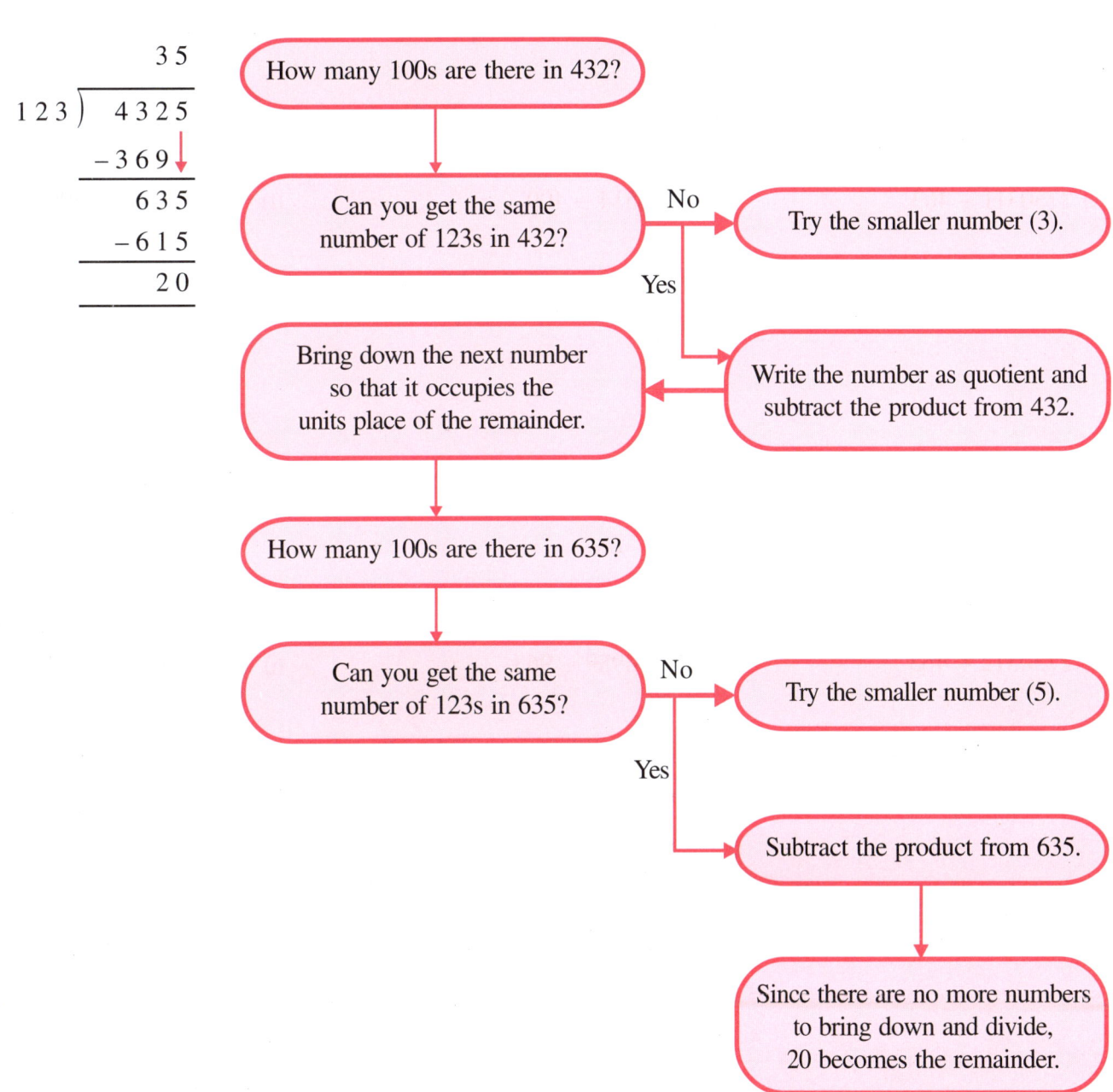

Exercise 7

Divide the following.

(a) 5638272 ÷ 324

(b) 190920 ÷ 215

(c) 6432750 ÷ 125

(d) 2730311 ÷ 463

(e) 550514 ÷ 409

(f) 13207876 ÷ 3509

(g) 2730312 ÷ 463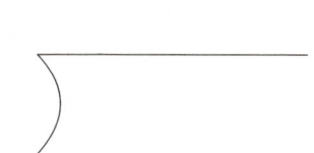

(h) 9394989 ÷ 963

(i) 282904694 ÷ 523

(j) 15995177 ÷ 584

(k) 94399662 ÷ 128

(l) 52134578 ÷ 125

(m) 2965950 ÷ 650

(n) 1528137 ÷ 333

(o) 1555642 ÷ 341

Vocabulary Learnt

operations   subtrahend   minuend

combining   rounding

family   addends   facts

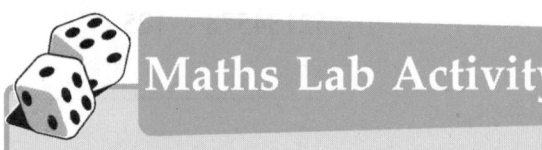
Maths Lab Activity 3

Materials required

(a) Blackboard (b) Chalk (c) Paper (d) Pencil

Method (Note for the Teacher)

Describe the activity to the students by writing the following instructions on the board.

Instructions

(a) Column A is for 'halving' and column B is for 'doubling'.

(b) Ignore the remainders in the halving column.

(c) Keep finding halves till you reach 1.

(d) Double the number of times you have halved in the adjacent column.

(e) Cross out all the numbers in column B which are opposite an even number in column A. Add up the numbers that remain in column B and that is your answer for the sum.

(f) Cross check by direct multiplication.

Example   23 × 45

Column A	Column B	
2 3	4 5	
1 1	9 0	
5	1 8 0	360 is the only number that is opposite
2	~~3 6 0~~	an even number. So, cancel it.
1 ────────▶	7 2 0	

Now, 45 + 90 + 180 + 720 = 1 0 3 5.

Check if 23 × 45 = 1035.

```
        2  3
    ×   4  5
    ─────────
        1  1  5
     9  2  0
    ─────────
  1  0  3  5
    ─────────
```

Now, solve the following and write your answer in the cloud.

(a) 34 × 67 =

(b) 56 × 97 =

Give different multiplication sentences and ask the students to find the answers by using the same method.

Maths Lab Activity 4

Palindromes

Materials required

(a) Blackboard   (b) Chalk   (c) Paper   (d) Pencil

Method (Note for the Teacher)

Explain to the students that palindromes are numbers that read the same backwards and forwards.

Example   34543

Write down all the steps that students should follow to get palindromes.

(a) First choose a number

(b) Then, reverse its digits to create a new number.

(c) Now, add the two numbers.

(d) You have your number palindrome!

```
   243
   342
   ___
   585
   ___
```

Note: Sometimes, repeated reversing and adding has to be done before getting the palindrome.

Look at this.
```
    169
    961
   1130
   0311
   ____
   1441
   ____
```

Ask the students to create five palindromes and copy them here in the space provided.

(a) _____   (b) _____   (c) _____   (d) _____   (e) _____

Chapter 4 — Test of Divisibility

> **You know...**
> - divisibility rules of 2, 3, 4, 5, 6, 8, 9 and 10.

You all know that division is one of the operations of Arithmetic. All the four operations have their own rules which help us to find answers to the given problems. Now, we will learn about the rules of division.

(a) The number to be divided is the dividend.

(b) The number you divide by is the divisor.

(c) The number of sets you get after dividing is the quotient.

(d) The number left over from the dividend is the remainder.

If a number is small, it is easy to find whether it is divisible by the given number or not. But, what do we do if we have to divide a large number by a divisor which is also large?

Division has its own rules which are used to find out whether the number is a divisor of a given number. These rules are called the test of divisibility.

You have already learnt the tests of divisibility of 2, 3, 4, 5, 6, 8, 9 and 10. So let us do a quick revision.

(a) **A number is divisible by 2 if the last digit is 0, 2, 4, 6 or 8.**

Colour all the clouds that have numbers divisible by 2 in green.

- 24983
- 69250
- 451864
- 981036
- 6700981

(b) **A number is divisible by 3 if the sum of the digits is divisible by 3.**

Colour all the clouds that have numbers divisible by 3 in red.

- 24983
- 700458
- 2345160
- 6594831
- 7145001

(c) **A number is divisible by 4 if the last two digits are 00 or are divisible by 4.**

Colour all the clouds that have numbers divisible by 4 in blue.

- 694123
- 542180
- 291361
- 243812
- 496888

(d) **A number is divisible by 5 if the last digit is 0 or 5.**

Colour all the clouds that have numbers divisible by 5 in yellow.

- 741895
- 235678
- 904070
- 7104089
- 8469123

(e) A number is divisible by 6 if the number is divisible by 2 and 3.

Colour all the clouds that have numbers divisible by 6 in pink.

7843212   9814600   6314934   3165783   7499873

(f) A number is divisible by 8 if the last three digits are divisible by 8.

Colour all the clouds that have numbers divisible by 8 in purple.

698104   784316   3890808   4136528   3470011

(g) A number is divisible by 9 if the sum of the digits is divisible by 9.

Colour all the clouds that have numbers divisible by 9 in brown.

6301485   7120844   6729984   2109680   6354126

(h) A numbers is divisible by 10 if the last digit is 0.

Colour all the numbers that are divisible by 10 in orange.

7498121   6350400   3418173   6942107   2407550

Maths Lab Activity 1

Material required

Several large flash cards with 6- or 7-digit number

Method (Note for the Teacher)

Ask the students to stand in a circle. Place one number card in front of each student. Tell them to run as you clap your hands and stop in front of a card when the clapping stops. They should pick up the card and find one divisor for the number by using the divisibility rule. Play the game several times so that they learn to find numbers for different rules.

Now, let us look at the rules for some other numbers.

Divisibility Rule for 7

Remove the last digit and double it. Subtract it from the remaining number. If the answer is 0 or a number divisible by 7, then the whole number is divisible by 7. You are actually subtracting multiples of 7. Continue the rule till you reach a smaller number where you can decide if the number is divisible by 7 or not.

Example   1274 – On applying the test, we get 127 – (2 × 4) = 119. This, when divided by 7, gives 17 as quotient and leaves no remainder. So, 1274 is divisible by 7.

Divisibility Rule for 11

A number is divisible by 11 when the difference between the sum of every digit in the odd place and every digit in the even place of a number is 0 or 11.

Example   496133

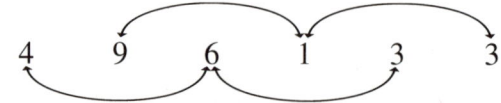

Sum of digits in the odd places = 4 + 6 + 3 =   13
Sum of digits in the even places = 9 + 1 + 3 = −13
                                                 0

Here the difference is zero. So, 496133 is divisible by 11.

Divisibility Rule for 12

A number is divisible by 12 if the sum of all its digits is divisible by 3 and the last two digits are divisible by 4.

Example   369240

(a) 3 + 6 + 9 + 2 + 4 + 0 = 24

   2 + 4 = 6

   6 is divisible by 3.

   So 369240 is divisible by 3.

(b) 369240

   40 is divisible by 4.

   So, 369240 is divisible by 4.

   Hence, the whole number 369240 is divisible by 12.

> **Remember!**
> If the number is divisible either by 3 or 4 alone, then it is not divisible by 12.

Divisibility Rule for 15

A number is divisible by 15 if the number is divisible by 3 and 5.

Example   483990

(a) 4 + 8 + 3 + 9 + 9 + 0 = 33

   3 + 3 = 6

   6 is divisible by 3. So 483990 is divisible by 15.

(b) 483990 is divisible by 5 as the last digit is 0.

> **Remember!**
> If the number is divisible by either 3 or 5 alone, then the number is not divisible by 15.

Divisibility Rule for 18

A number is divisible by 18 if the number is divisible by 2 and 9.

Example 2436426

(a) 2436426 is divisible by 2 as the last digit is 2.

(b) 2 + 4 + 3 + 6 + 4 + 2 + 6 = 27
2 + 7 = 9
9 is divisible by 9. So 2436426 is also divisible by 18.

Divisibility Rule for 25

A number is divisible by 25 if the last two digits are zeroes or are divisible by 25.

Example 1 2987600

(b) The last two digits are 00.
So 2987600 is also divisible by 25.

Example 2 4724850

(a) The last two digits of this number are 5 and 0, which make 50. 50 is divisible by 25.
So 4724850 is divisible by 25.

Exercise 1

(a) Which of these numbers are divisible by 7?
   (i) 438561   (ii) 562632   (iii) 654320   (iv) 141701   (v) 598752

(b) Which of these numbers are divisible by 11?
   (i) 438169   (ii) 2944821   (iii) 67843   (iv) 123244   (v) 731698

(c) Which of these numbers are divisible by 12?
   (i) 36940   (ii) 63180   (iii) 504379   (iv) 479160   (v) 127296

(d) Which of these numbers are divisible by 15?
   (i) 937950   (ii) 751695   (iii) 413896   (iv) 247515   (v) 694871

(e) Which of these numbers are divisible by 18?
   (i) 321098   (ii) 341269   (iii) 650916   (iv) 700213   (v) 912600

(f) Which of these numbers are divisible by 25?
   (i) 4876500   (ii) 298475   (iii) 1470250   (iv) 6741890   (v) 7290416

Exercise 2

(a) What would you add to the following as the last digit to make them divisible by 3?

  (i) 4976 ___   (ii) 2184 ___   (iii) 8509 ___

(b) What would you add to the following as the last digit to make them divisible by 4?

  (i) 13678 ___   (ii) 59843 ___   (iii) 67210 ___

(c) What would you add to the following as the last digit to make them divisible by 6?

  (i) 29841 ___   (ii) 98463 ___   (iii) 410082 ___

(d) What would you add to the following as the last digit to make them divisible by 8?

  (i) 234140 ___   (ii) 567021 ___   (iii) 900876 ___

(e) What would you add to the following as the last digit to make them divisible by 9?

  (i) 269143 ___   (ii) 408721 ___   (iii) 581949 ___

(f) What would you add to the following as the last digit to make them divisible by 11?

  (i) 23469 ___   (ii) 43129 ___

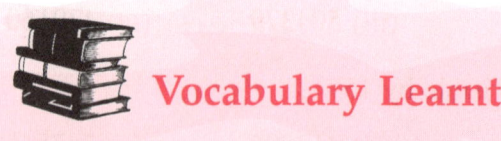

Vocabulary Learnt

divisibility   quotient   remainder

remove   rule

double   dividend   divisor

Chapter 5 — Powers of Numbers

> **You know...**
> - a number multiplied by itself will give a square number
> - a number multiplied three times by itself will give a cube number
> - to find area of a square, you multiply a number by itself
> - to find the volume of a cube, you multiply a number three times by itself.

A number written a little raised next to a number is the **power** of the number. It is also called the **index** or the **exponent**. The index should be written in a smaller size. It shows the number of times a number is multiplied by itself.

For example, 3^5. Here 3 is called the **base number** and 5 is called its **index**. In other words, it means 3 is multiplied 5 times by itself. ($3 \times 3 \times 3 \times 3 \times 3 = 243$).

Exercise 1

(a) Write the exponential form in the given boxes.

Example $4 \times 4 \times 4 = \boxed{4^3}$

(i) $6 \times 6 \times 6 \times 6 =$ ☐
(ii) $7 \times 7 \times 7 \times 7 \times 7 \times 7 =$ ☐
(iii) $9 \times 9 \times 9 \times 9 \times 9 \times 9 \times 9 =$ ☐
(iv) $2 \times 2 \times 2 \times 2 \times 2 \times 2 \times 2 \times 2 =$ ☐
(v) $5 \times 5 \times 5 \times 5 \times 5 \times 5 \times 5 =$ ☐
(vi) $4 \times 4 \times 4 \times 4 \times 4 \times 4 \times 4 \times 4 \times 4 =$ ☐
(vi) $3 \times 3 \times 3 \times 3 \times 3 \times 3 =$ ☐
(viii) $8 \times 8 \times 8 \times 8 \times 8 \times 8 \times 8 \times 8 \times 8 =$ ☐
(ix) $5 \times 5 \times 5 \times 5 =$ ☐
(x) $7 \times 7 \times 7 \times 7 \times 7 =$ ☐

(b) Write in expanded form to show how many times each one of these numbers has been multiplied.

Example $6^3 = 6 \times 6 \times 6$ (3 times)

(i) 7^9 ———
(ii) 6^3 ———
(iii) 3^2 ———
(iv) 7^5 ———
(v) 9^2 ———
(vi) 6^7 ———
(vi) 8^4 ———
(viii) 7^5 ———
(ix) 9^5 ———
(x) 12^4 ———

(c) Match the value with the numbers by colouring them alike.

2^3 3125   343   128 6^4 4^4

The first power is the number itself.

3^5 10,000 4^2 2^7 1296 2^2

The second power is the square of the number.

8   512 8^3 5^5 16 3^6

The third power is the cube of the number.

10^4 4 7^3 256   243   729

(d) Find the value and arrange the numbers in ascending order.

| $2^3 =$ | $3^4 =$ | $7^2 =$ |

| $6^2 =$ | $5^3 =$ | $2^9 =$ |

| $4^3 =$ | $2^6 =$ | $3^5 =$ |

(e) Find the value and arrange the numbers in descending order.

| $4^3 =$ | $6^2 =$ | $5^2 =$ |

| $4^2 =$ | $3^4 =$ | $5^3 =$ |

| $9^2 =$ | $7^3 =$ | $8^2 =$ |

Prime Factor Method

You have already learnt how to find the prime factors of a number. When you have found them out, they can be grouped together and written in exponential form. If a factor is not repeated even once, then write it as it is.

Example 1   125

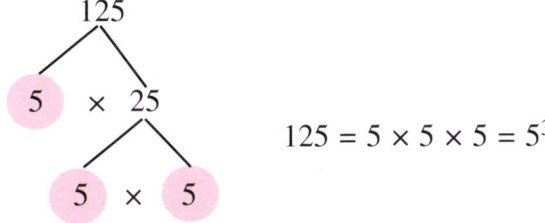

$125 = 5 \times 5 \times 5 = 5^3$

Example 2   600

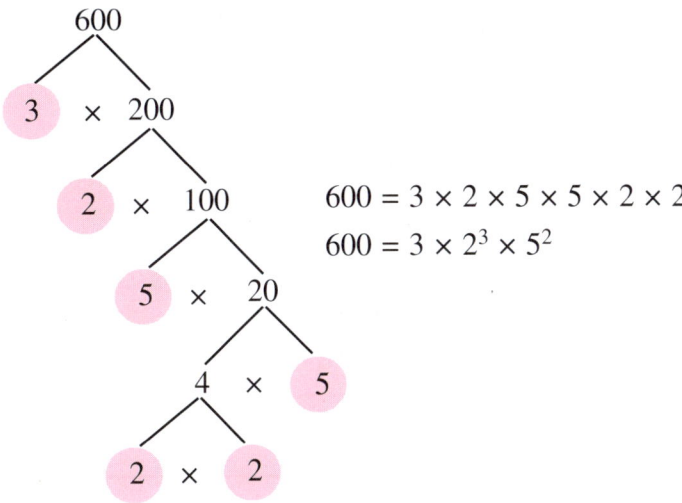

$600 = 3 \times 2 \times 5 \times 5 \times 2 \times 2$

$600 = 3 \times 2^3 \times 5^2$

Exercise 2

Now solve the following.

(a) 240

(b) 365

(c) 625

(d) 352

Division Method to Find the Power

Example

```
5 | 120
2 | 24
2 | 12
2 | 6
3 | 3
  | 1
```

$120 = 5 \times 2 \times 2 \times 2 \times 3 = 5 \times 3 \times 2^3$

Exercise 3

(a) Now solve the following in your notebook.

(i) 456   (ii) 450   (iii) 342   (iv) 786   (v) 620   (vi) 780
(vii) 875   (viii) 532   (ix) 654   (x) 237   (xi) 324   (xii) 915

Exercise 4

Example $2^2 \times 4^2 = \underbrace{2 \times 2}_{4} \times \underbrace{4 \times 4}_{16} = 64$

Now expand the following.

(a) $6^3 \times 5^2$ _____

(b) $4^6 \times 2^3$ _____

(c) $5^3 \times 6^2$ _____

(d) $6^4 \times 8^3$ _____

(e) $5^2 \times 7^3$ _____

(f) $7^4 \times 8^2$ _____

(g) $9^2 \times 6^3$ _____

(h) $7^3 \times 6^5$ _____

(i) $10^3 \times 7^3$ _____

(j) $7^4 \times 5^4$ _____

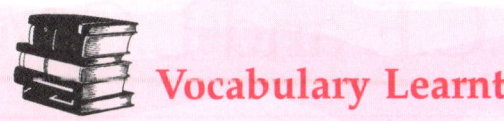

Vocabulary Learnt

index	power	exponent
	value	form
square	cube	raise

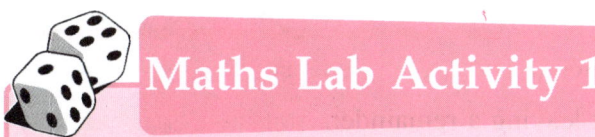

Maths Lab Activity 1

Material required

(a) Large flash cards with numbers in exponential form

(b) Cards with their values when multiplied, like the ones given below

Method (Note for the Teacher)

Keep the cards with the exponential numbers with you. Ask the students to sit in pairs. Distribute the value cards, one to each group. Call out the numbers in one card, say $3^4 \times 2^4$. All the groups will solve the numbers in exponential form. The group with the card having 1296 should stand up and show their card. Repeat the activity till all get a chance to participate.

$5^2 \times 2^3$	25
$9^2 + 6^2$	7751
$6^5 - 5^2$	54
$8^3 - 2^3$	504
$7^3 \times 4^2$	200
$10^3 + 5^3$	117
$5^4 \div 5^2$	1125

Chapter 6 — H.C.F. and L.C.M.

> **You know...**
> - the meaning of factors and multiples
> - a number can have several factors and multiples
> - multiples are infinite, while factors are limited
> - two or more numbers can have common factors and multiples
> - factors and multiples have a relationship.

You have already learnt what a factor is. Let us do a quick review.

A factor is a number that can divide another number without leaving a remainder.

Look at this.

24 is divisible by 2, 3, 4, 6, 8, 12 and 24.

So all these are factors of 24. In other words, 24 is a multiple of all these numbers because 24 comes in the multiplication tables of these numbers.

Look at this.

```
 2 – 2, 4, 6, 8, 10, 12, 14, 16, 18, 20, 22, [24]
 3 – 3, 6, 9, 12, 15, 18, 21, [24]
 4 – 4, 8, 12, 16, 20, [24]
 6 – 6, 12, 18, [24]
 8 – 8, 16, [24]
12 – 12, [24]
24 – [24]
```

Maths Lab Activity 1

Material required

Several number cards

Method (Note for the Teacher)

Give each student a number card and ask the students to give a multiple as well as a factor of the number on the card. For example, if one gets the number 45, he/she can say 9 is a factor and 90 is a multiple.

Give slightly bigger and challenging numbers. This helps them to use their tables as well as the divisibility rules.

Highest Common Factor (H.C.F.)

To find the Highest Common Factor, we need to look at the factors of two or more numbers. There are two or three different ways of finding the factors.

Method 1

Factor Method

$20 =$ 2, 4, 5, 10, 20
$24 =$ 2, 3, 4, 6, 8, 12, 24

2 and 4 are the common factors, but 4 is the greater of the two. So, H.C.F. of 20 and 24 = 4.

Method 2

Tree Method (Prime Factorisation)

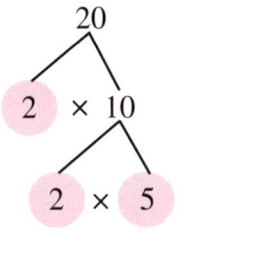
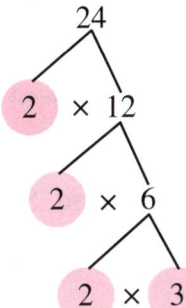

$20 = 2 \times 2 \times 5$
$24 = 2 \times 2 \times 2 \times 3$

Here, you take the common factors and multiply them together. So $2 \times 2 = 4$.
Hence, H.C.F. of 20 and 24 = 4.

Method 3

Division Method

```
2 | 20        2 | 24
2 | 10        3 | 12
5 |  5        2 |  4
     1        2 |  2
                   1
```

$20 = 2 \times 5 \times 2$
$24 = 2 \times 3 \times 2 \times 2$

Again take the common factors and multiply them together: $2 \times 2 = 4$.
So, the H.C.F. of 20 and 24 is 4.

Method 4

Long Division Method

Step 1: Divide the greater number by the smaller number and find the remainder.
Step 2: Divide the smaller number or the divisor by the remainder.
Step 3: Continue till you reach the last divisor. It is the H.C.F.

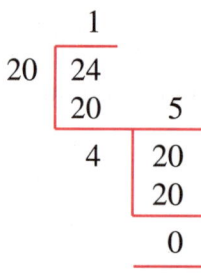

So, H.C.F. of 20 and 24 is 4.

Method 5

Using the Rule of Divisibility

Divide the two numbers by a common factor, which should be a prime number. Here, 2 divides 20 and 24, and you get 10 and 12 respectively. Again, 2 divides 10 and 12 and you get 5 and 6. Now, no number will divide both 5 and 6. So, stop now and multiply the divisors used so far to get the H.C.F. = 2 × 2 = 4.

```
2 | 20, 24
2 | 10, 12
    5,  6
```

So, H.C.F. of 20 and 24 = 4

You already know the tree method and the short division method. So try these.

Exercise 1

Find the H.C.F. using long division.

(a) 92, 64   (b) 90, 110   (c) 216, 124

(d) 124, 216   (e) 150, 225   (f) 75, 250

Exercise 2

Find the H.C.F. using the rule of divisibility.

(a) 24, 76   (b) 45, 75   (c) 34, 78

(d) 98, 120   (e) 131, 231   (f) 280, 476

Least Common Multiple (L.C.M.)

You have already learnt about multiples in your previous class. Let us do a quick review of it.

Multiples are numbers that make up the multiplication table of a number. Every number has multiples, which are infinite in number.

Look at this.

12, 24, 36, 48 and so on are the multiples of 12.

You can find the multiples of a number by multiplying it with other whole numbers. Some numbers share multiples.

Look at this.

Multiples of 6 = ⑥, ⑫, ⑱, 24, 30, 36

Multiples of 3 = 3, ⑥, 9, ⑫, 15, ⑱

You will notice that 6, 12, and 18 are multiples shared by 3 and 6.

If you continue finding more multiples, there will be more common multiples. The least multiple, which is common for two or more numbers, is their Least Common Multiple or L.C.M.

There are many ways of finding the Least Common Multiple. Let us look at them.

Method 1

Multiples Method

As mentioned above, you can keep on finding the multiples of both the numbers till you get a common one. Check with the first 5 or 6 multiples first. If you do not find a common multiple, continue till the next five or six multiples.

Example   L.C.M. of 8 and 10

Multiples of 8 = 8, 16, 24, 32, 40, 48, ...

Multiples of 10 = 10, 20, 30, 40, ...

40 is the first common multiple of 8 and 10. So, L.C.M. of 8 and 10 = 40.

Exercise 3

Find the L.C.M. using the multiples method.

(a) 12 and 15   (b) 30 and 45

(c) 12, 15 and 18   (d) 20, 50, 75

Method 2

Division Method

You can find the L.C.M. by division method also.

Step 1: Divide the numbers by a prime number.
Step 2: If a number cannot be divided by the chosen prime number, bring it down and divide separately.
Step 3: Continue till the two numbers have 1 as their quotient.
Step 4: Multiply all the divisors together to get the L.C.M.

Example   L.C.M. of 8 and 10

$$\begin{array}{r|rr} 2 & 8, & 10 \\ \hline 2 & 4, & 5 \\ \hline 2 & 2, & 5 \\ \hline 5 & 1, & 5 \\ \hline & 1, & 1 \end{array}$$

L.C.M. = 2 × 2 × 2 × 5 = 40.

Exercise 4

Find the L.C.M. using the division method.

(a) 93, 62 and 120   (b) 11, 22 and 55

(c) 15, 20 and 18   (d) 39, 66 and 45

Method 3

Prime Factorisation Method

This is also known as the **tree method**.
Step 1: Find any two factors individually for the given numbers.
Step 2: Again find factors for those numbers.

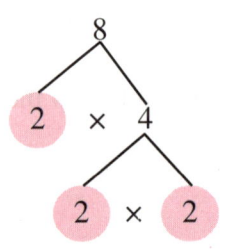
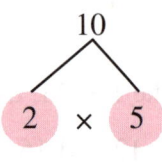

Step 3: Continue to find factors until all are prime numbers.
Step 4: Group the common factors of the two numbers.
Step 5: Take every common factor and uncommon factor, and multiply to get the L.C.M.

$8 = \boxed{2} \times 2 \times 2$ The 2 in the box is the common factor. The uncommon factors are 2, 2 and 5.
$10 = \boxed{2} \times 5$ So, multiply $2 \times 2 \times 2 \times 5 = 40$. Therefore, L.C.M. = 40.

Exercise 5

Find the L.C.M. by prime factorisation method.

(a) 28 and 48

(b) 12 and 16

(c) 22 and 66

(d) 75 and 100

(e) 48 and 72

(f) 76 and 57

(g) 50 and 80

(h) 30 and 70

Relationship between H.C.F. and L.C.M.

Look at this.

Find the H.C.F. and L.C.M. of 20 and 24.

H.C.F. = 4 and L.C.M. = 120.

What is the product of the two numbers? (480)

What is the product of the H.C.F. and L.C.M.? (480)

You will notice that the product of the two numbers is equal to the product of their H.C.F. and L.C.M.

So L.C.M. = $\dfrac{\text{Product of the two numbers}}{\text{H.C.F.}}$ and H.C.F. = $\dfrac{\text{Product of the two numbers}}{\text{L.C.M.}}$.

It is also possible to find one of the two numbers if the other number and the H.C.F. and L.C.M. are given.

Example H.C.F. = 5, L.C.M. = 60 and one of the numbers is 15. What is the other number?

Assume, the unknown number is 'y'.

$$15 \times y = 5 \times 60. \text{ (You already know this.)}$$

(a) You have to take 'y' separately to find its value.

(b) To separate it, you have to divide the constant (number) on the left by itself.

(c) Whatever you do to the left side, you have to do to the right side also, in order to keep the value same.

So you get,

$y = \dfrac{5 \times 60}{15} = \dfrac{300}{15} = 20$ So the other number is 20.

Exercise 6

Find the L.C.M.

(a) The product of two numbers = 180. H.C.F. = 5.

(b) The product of two numbers = 500. H.C.F. = 100.

(c) The product of two numbers = 252. H.C.F. = 2.

(d) The product of two numbers is = 1260. H.C.F. = 6.

Exercise 7

Find the H.C.F.

(a) The product of two numbers = 375. L.C.M. = 75.

(b) The product of two numbers = 240. L.C.M. = 240.

(c) The product of two numbers = 3456. L.C.M. = 144.

(d) The product of two numbers = 9600. L.C.M. = 120.

Word Attack

(a) There are 20 red and 24 green pencils in a shop. The shopkeeper wants to distribute them equally in boxes. Find the largest number of pencils that can be put in each box.

(b) There are 4 poles measuring 105 cm, 120 cm, 125 cm and 140 cm. If they have to be arranged into pieces of equal length, what is the maximum length they have to be cut into?

(c) There are 105, 126 and 213 mangoes on 3 trees. What is the largest group into which the mangoes can be split, if they have to be arranged equally?

(d) Raju, Steven and Anwar start walking at speeds of 3 km/hr, 4 km/hr and 5 km/hr respectively. When will the three first meet again at one place, if they are following the same route?

(e) What will be the capacity of the smallest drum which can be filled completely using each of the cups that can fill exactly 75 ml, 200 ml and 140 ml?

(f) Four buses leave Chennai at the same time. The first bus is seen after 3 hours, the second after 4 hours, the third after 5 hours and the fourth after 6 hours. After how many hours from the starting time, will all of them come together?

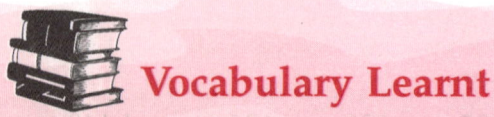

Vocabulary Learnt

factor   common   multiple

prime   infinite

divisibility   relationship   factorisation

Chapter 7

Fractions

> **You know...**
> - a fraction is a part of a whole
> - a fraction has two terms – a numerator and a denominator
> - a whole can be just one unit or a group of objects taken as one unit
> - a fraction can be proper or improper.

Let us quickly revise what we have learnt about fractions in the previous class.

Exercise 1

(a) Express the following mixed numbers as improper fractions.

(i) $12\frac{2}{3}$ ___   (ii) $18\frac{2}{5}$ ___   (iii) $4\frac{1}{8}$ ___

(iv) $6\frac{3}{4}$ ___   (v) $12\frac{3}{12}$ ___   (vi) $3\frac{3}{11}$ ___

(b) Express the following improper fractions as mixed numbers.

(i) $\frac{14}{3}$ ___   (ii) $\frac{29}{7}$ ___   (iii) $\frac{49}{8}$ ___

(iv) $\frac{120}{11}$ ___   (v) $\frac{115}{10}$ ___   (vi) $\frac{53}{6}$ ___

(c) Reduce to the lowest term.

(i) $\frac{16}{24}$ ___   (ii) $\frac{13}{39}$ ___   (iii) $\frac{120}{200}$ ___

(iv) $\frac{44}{143}$ ___   (v) $\frac{100}{250}$ ___   (vi) $\frac{99}{171}$ ___

(d) Use < or > sign.

(i) $\frac{2}{3}$ ◯ $\frac{4}{5}$ (ii) $\frac{6}{9}$ ◯ $\frac{2}{7}$ (iii) $\frac{5}{8}$ ◯ $\frac{7}{11}$

(iv) $\frac{7}{12}$ ◯ $\frac{11}{13}$ (v) $\frac{6}{9}$ ◯ $\frac{7}{8}$ (vi) $\frac{6}{7}$ ◯ $\frac{2}{9}$

(e) Arrange in ascending order.

(i) $\frac{3}{4}, \frac{5}{9}, \frac{1}{2}, \frac{5}{6}$ ☐

(ii) $\frac{2}{3}, \frac{1}{8}, \frac{4}{5}, \frac{2}{4}$ ☐

(f) Arrange in descending order.

(i) $\frac{6}{9}, \frac{4}{5}, \frac{1}{3}, \frac{2}{8}$ ☐

(ii) $\frac{2}{3}, \frac{2}{8}, \frac{2}{5}, \frac{1}{4}$ ☐

Maths Lab Activity 1

Materials required

(a) A set of cards showing mixed numbers
(b) A set of cards showing corresponding improper fractions
(c) A set of cards showing corresponding diagrams

Samples of these are given below.

Method (Note for the Teacher)

Divide the students into three groups. Give the improper fractions to one group, the mixed numbers to the second group and the diagrams to the third group.

Ask a student from any group to stand up and show his card. Students from the other two groups who have the corresponding cards must stand up and show their cards. Check to see if all three are the same. Continue till all get a chance. If time permits, ask the groups to exchange their cards and play again.

$2\frac{5}{7}$	$\frac{19}{7}$	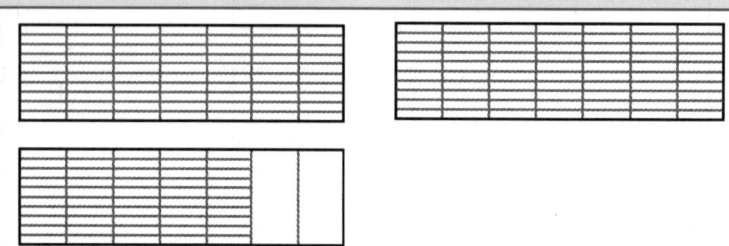
$3\frac{1}{5}$	$\frac{16}{5}$	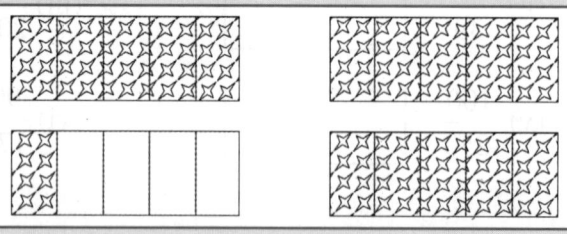
$3\frac{2}{4}$	$\frac{14}{4}$	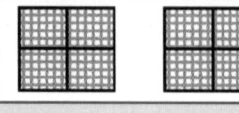 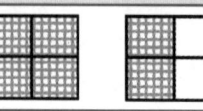
$3\frac{1}{3}$	$\frac{10}{3}$	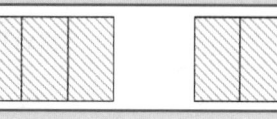 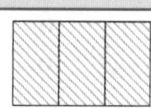 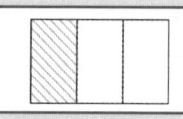

Multiplication of Fractions

Multiplication of fractions can be shown by using rows and columns. Their meeting points give the answer.

Example

$$\frac{1}{3} \times \frac{1}{4}$$

Rows × columns

Step 1: Draw a box. Divide it into three horizontal equal parts. These are called rows. Shade one row to represent $\frac{1}{3}$.

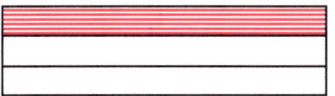

Step 2: Divide the box into four vertical equal parts. These are called columns. Shade one column to represent $\frac{1}{4}$.

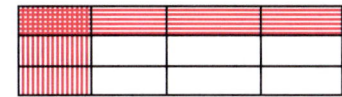

Find out how many shaded boxes are overlapped. That gives the numerator of your answer. (Here, only one box is overlapped.)

How many boxes are there in all now? (There are 12 boxes in all.) That is the denominator of your answer.

So $\frac{1}{3} \times \frac{1}{4} = \frac{1}{12}$.

You will notice here that you multiply the two numerators and the two denominators to get the answer.

Exercise 2

Draw equal-sized boxes to get the product of the given fractions. Instead of drawing lines, use two different colours to shade the boxes.

(a) $\frac{1}{4} \times \frac{1}{5}$

(b) $\frac{2}{4} \times \frac{1}{3}$

(c) $\dfrac{1}{5} \times \dfrac{1}{7}$

(d) $\dfrac{2}{5} \times \dfrac{2}{3}$

You can also multiply without using the diagrams and find the answer.

Example $\quad \dfrac{1}{3} \times \dfrac{4}{5} = \dfrac{4}{15}$

Exercise 3

Multiply the following fractions. Write your answer in the boxes provided.

(a) $\dfrac{3}{5} \times \dfrac{1}{6} = \boxed{}$
(b) $\dfrac{2}{5} \times \dfrac{4}{7} = \boxed{}$
(c) $\dfrac{2}{6} \times \dfrac{7}{9} = \boxed{}$
(d) $\dfrac{5}{7} \times \dfrac{2}{6} = \boxed{}$

(e) $\dfrac{4}{8} \times \dfrac{2}{4} = \boxed{}$
(f) $\dfrac{1}{6} \times \dfrac{2}{8} = \boxed{}$
(g) $\dfrac{2}{3} \times \dfrac{4}{5} = \boxed{}$
(h) $\dfrac{4}{6} \times \dfrac{7}{8} = \boxed{}$

(i) $\dfrac{5}{8} \times \dfrac{3}{9} = \boxed{}$
(j) $\dfrac{3}{7} \times \dfrac{2}{5} = \boxed{}$
(k) $\dfrac{6}{9} \times \dfrac{6}{8} = \boxed{}$
(l) $\dfrac{4}{6} \times \dfrac{2}{7} = \boxed{}$

Division of Fractions

You know division means to separate something into equal groups or to share equally. It is also the opposite of multiplication. When you multiply, you gather equal groups together. When you divide, you split the collection into equal groups.

You cannot divide by a fraction, as it has two terms. So, change the fraction into a whole number first. To get the whole number, multiply the given fraction by its reciprocal. For example, the reciprocal of 3/1 is 1/3. To divide fractions, change the operation to multiplication and then multiply.

Dividing a Whole Number by a Fraction

Example

$3 \div \dfrac{1}{3}$

Step 1: Here 3 is a whole number that has to be divided by $\dfrac{1}{3}$.

$\dfrac{3}{1} \div \dfrac{1}{3} = \dfrac{\frac{3}{1}}{\frac{1}{3}}$

Step 2: To convert the denominator into a whole number, multiply it with its reciprocal. Multiply the numerator with the same so that the value of the fraction does not change.

$$\frac{\frac{3}{1} \times \frac{3}{1}}{\frac{1}{3} \times \frac{3}{1}} = \frac{\frac{9}{1}}{\frac{3}{3}} = \frac{\frac{9}{1}}{\frac{1}{1}} = \frac{9}{1}$$

Cancel the 1 and take only $\frac{9}{1}$.

$\frac{9}{1} = 9$ So, 9 is the answer.

Exercise 4

Divide the whole number by the fraction.

(a) $9 \div \frac{1}{3}$ (b) $8 \div \frac{2}{4}$ (c) $6 \div \frac{1}{3}$

(d) $4 \div \frac{1}{2}$ (e) $12 \div \frac{1}{3}$ (f) $2 \div \frac{1}{5}$

(g) $7 \div \frac{1}{3}$ (h) $14 \div \frac{1}{7}$ (i) $6 \div \frac{4}{5}$

Dividing a Fraction by a Fraction

To divide two fractional numbers, multiply the dividend fraction with the inverse of the divisor fractions.

Example

$$\frac{1}{4} \div \frac{2}{3} \qquad \left(\frac{1}{4} \times \frac{3}{2} = \frac{3}{8} \right)$$

$$= \frac{\frac{1}{4}}{\frac{2}{3}} = \frac{\frac{1}{4} \times \frac{3}{2}}{\frac{2}{3} \times \frac{3}{2}} = \frac{\frac{3}{8}}{\frac{6}{6}} = \frac{\frac{3}{8}}{1} = \text{So } \frac{3}{8} \text{ is the answer.}$$

> **Remember!**
> The denominator of whole numbers is always 1.

Exercise 5

Now divide the fraction by another fraction.

(a) $\dfrac{4}{5} \div \dfrac{3}{8}$

(b) $\dfrac{6}{9} \div \dfrac{5}{6}$

(c) $\dfrac{3}{8} \div \dfrac{5}{9}$

(d) $\dfrac{2}{5} \div \dfrac{1}{5}$

(e) $\dfrac{1}{4} \div \dfrac{15}{3}$

(f) $\dfrac{3}{4} \div \dfrac{7}{2}$

(g) $\dfrac{4}{6} \div \dfrac{4}{9}$

(h) $\dfrac{5}{8} \div \dfrac{8}{5}$

(i) $\dfrac{2}{3} \div \dfrac{1}{4}$

Dividing a Fraction by a Whole Number

Example

$$\dfrac{2}{4} \div 5 = \dfrac{\dfrac{2}{4}}{\dfrac{5}{1}}$$

$$= \dfrac{\dfrac{2}{4} \times \dfrac{1}{5}}{\dfrac{5}{1} \times \dfrac{1}{5}} = \dfrac{\dfrac{2}{20}}{\dfrac{5}{5}}$$

$$= \dfrac{\dfrac{2}{20}}{\dfrac{1}{1}}$$

Remember to reduce the fraction to its lowest term.

$$= \dfrac{2 \div 2}{20 \div 2} = \dfrac{1}{10} \text{ is the answer.}$$

Exercise 6

Divide the fraction by the given whole number.

(a) $\dfrac{4}{6} \div 2$ (b) $\dfrac{3}{9} \div 5$ (c) $\dfrac{8}{10} \div 7$

(d) $\dfrac{6}{7} \div 8$ (e) $\dfrac{1}{5} \div 6$ (f) $\dfrac{5}{8} \div 8$

(g) $\dfrac{1}{5} \div 3$ (h) $\dfrac{1}{4} \div 12$ (i) $\dfrac{2}{7} \div 2$

Exercise 7

Tick the correct answer.

(a) $\dfrac{3}{4}$ of a dozen

    (i) 8   (ii) 9    (iii) 6

(b) $\dfrac{1}{2}$ of a century

    (i) 50    (ii) 25    (iii) 75

(c) $1\dfrac{1}{2}$ m

    (i) 124 cm   (ii) 100 cm   (iii) 150 cm

(d) $1\frac{1}{4}$ is half of

   (i) 3 ☐   (ii) $2\frac{1}{2}$ ☐   (iii) $2\frac{3}{4}$ ☐

(e) $\frac{1}{4}$ of a year

   (i) 4 months ☐   (ii) 3 months ☐   (iii) 6 months ☐

(f) $\frac{4}{5}$ of a rupee

   (i) 90 p ☐   (ii) 60 p ☐   (iii) 80 p ☐

(g) $\frac{1}{4}$ of a minute

   (i) 15 sec ☐   (ii) 18 sec ☐   (iii) 20 sec ☐

(h) $\frac{1}{3}$ of a day

   (i) 18 hours ☐   (ii) 10 hours ☐   (iii) 8 hours ☐

(i) $\frac{2}{5}$ of a kg

   (i) 500 g ☐   (ii) 400 g ☐   (iii) 350 g ☐

(j) $\frac{1}{2}$ a litre

   (i) 500 ml ☐   (ii) 550 ml ☐   (iii) 450 ml ☐

Word Attack

(a) Raju had 600 apples in his orchard. $\frac{1}{2}$ of them were ripe. So he plucked them and took them home. A shopkeeper took $\frac{1}{4}$ of the apples to sell. Raju sent the rest to the market. Due to the heat, $\frac{1}{5}$ of the remaining apples got spoilt. How many apples was he able to sell in the market?

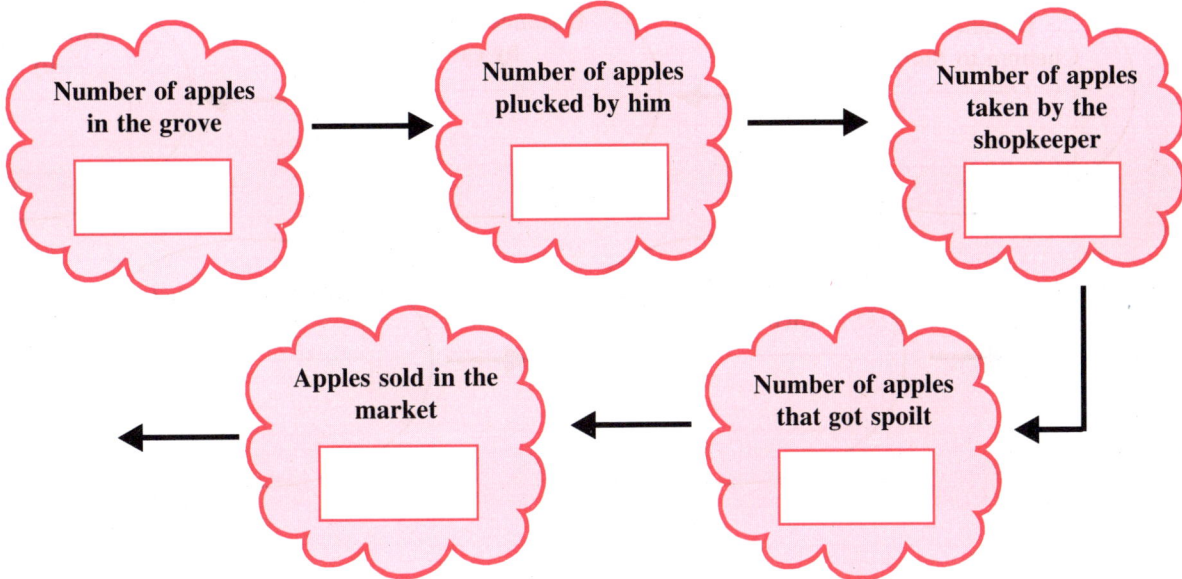

(b) Out of the total strength of 168 students in a school, $\frac{2}{3}$ were boys and $\frac{1}{2}$ of the girls lived in the hostel. During the Dussehra holidays, only $\frac{2}{7}$ of the girls went home. $\frac{1}{4}$ of the remaining girls took permission to stay with their friends or guardians in the city. How many girls stayed back in the hostel?

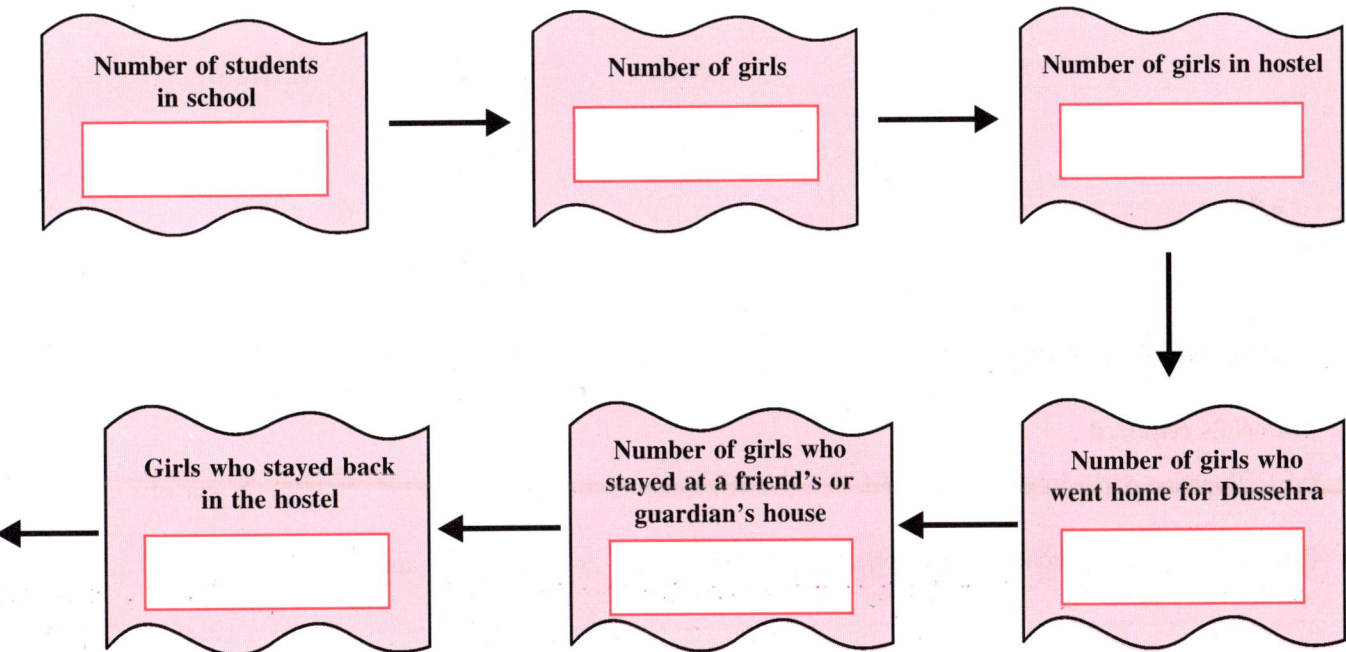

(c) The distance between Chennai and Bangalore is 320 km. Raghav covered half of the distance by car with a friend who was going to Ranipet. He was able to cover only $\frac{1}{4}$ of the remaining distance by bus, as it broke down on the way. He met a motorcyclist on the way with whom he travelled $\frac{3}{4}$ of the remaining distance. How much distance was left for him to reach his destination?

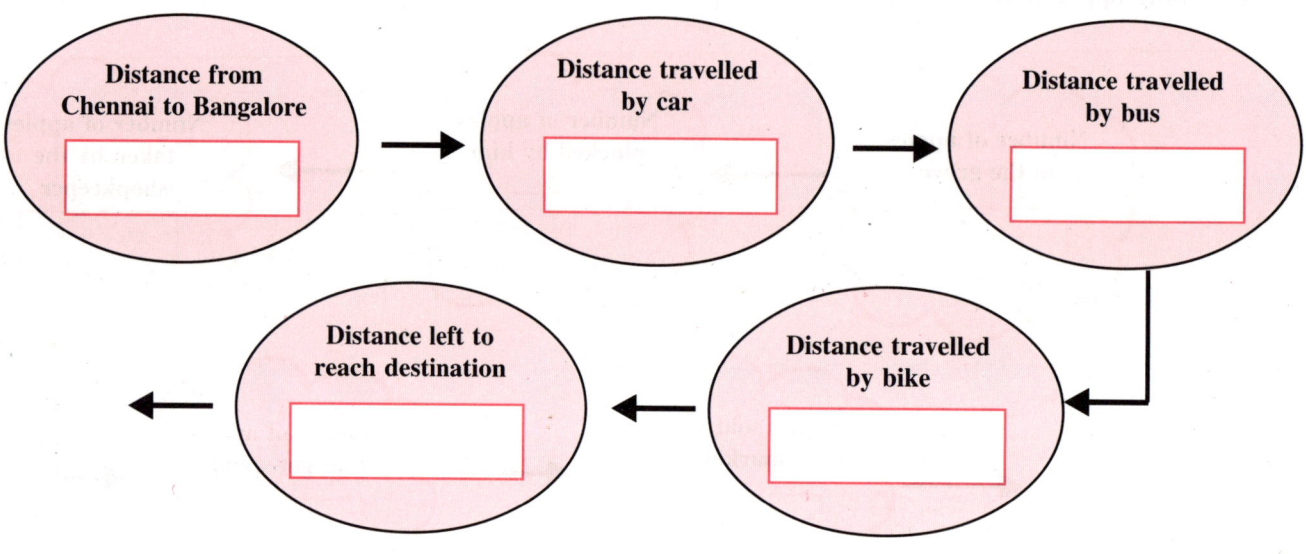

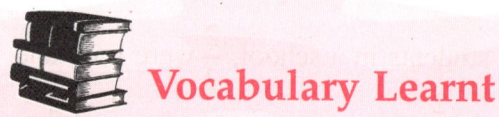

Vocabulary Learnt

columns   numerator   denominator
    reciprocal   horizontal
rows   reduce   vertical

Maths Lab Activity 2

Multiplication of fraction

Materials required

(a) Cellophane paper in yellow and red   (b) Glue to stick the papers   (c) A pair of scissors

(b) A sheet of paper each with multiplication problems like $\frac{1}{8} \times \frac{1}{5}$, $\frac{2}{6} \times \frac{3}{4}$ and so on

Method (Note for the Teacher)

Ask students to read the given problems carefully. Make them draw the boxes. Ask them to cut and stick the red cellophane paper on the required parts, shown by the first numerators and the yellow cellophane paper on the parts, shown by the second numerator. They will find out how many parts have turned orange and how many parts are there in all. The first number shows the rows and the second number shows columns.

(a) $\dfrac{4}{5} \times \dfrac{1}{2}$

(b) $\dfrac{3}{5} \times \dfrac{1}{4}$

(c) $\dfrac{2}{3} \times \dfrac{2}{6}$

(d) $\dfrac{1}{3} \times \dfrac{4}{5}$

Chapter 8 — Decimals

You know...

- decimals and fractions mean a part of a whole
- there can be any number of digits after a decimal point but their value together remains less than one
- the numbers after the point are read independent of each other
- you can perform all the four operations with decimals too.

Maths Lab Activity 1

Materials required

(a) Set of 0 to 9 number cards for each student
(b) Cards with decimal points (.) only

Method (Note for the Teacher)

Ask the students to sit in a circle and keep their number cards and point cards face down in front of them. Ask them to place the cards in some order, with the point card somewhere in between. Make them read the decimal numbers. Ensure that they read correctly (like four point three seven and not four point thirty seven).

| 4 | . | 3 | 7 |

You have learnt about decimals in the earlier class. So let us do a quick review.

Conversion of Decimals into Fractions

Example

$3.7 = \dfrac{37}{10}$ because the first place after the point is the tenth place.

$2.56 = \dfrac{256}{100}$ because second place after decimal point indicates hundredths.

$4.600 = \dfrac{4600}{1000}$ because third place after decimal point indicates thousandths.

Exercise 1

(a) Convert to fractions.

(i) 4.89 = (ii) 4.809 = (iii) 6.008 = (iv) 89.098 = (v) 2.555 = (vi) 8.12 =

(b) Convert to decimals.

(i) $4\dfrac{1}{10} =$

(ii) $56\dfrac{2}{100} =$

(iii) $678\dfrac{3}{1000} =$

(iv) $789\dfrac{3}{100} =$

(v) $78\dfrac{45}{1000} =$

Exercise 2

Change the given decimals to like decimals in the space provided.

To change unlike decimals to like decimals, add the required number of zeroes at the end wherever necessary to make all numbers have the same number of digits after the point.

Example   2.3, 34.58, 1.345 | 2.300, 34.580, 1.345 |

(a) 2.89, 34.678, 1.111, 7.8

(b) 2.45, 56.890, 2.1

(c) 4.78, 9.9, 12.1

Exercise 3

Example $234.789 = 200 + 30 + 4 + \dfrac{7}{10} + \dfrac{8}{100} + \dfrac{9}{1000}$

Write the following in expanded form.

(a) 34.678 =

(b) 5.908 =

(c) 23.126 =

(d) 678.786 =

(e) 5.006 =

(f) 34.008 =

Exercise 4

Example $200 + 50 + 7 + \dfrac{6}{10} + \dfrac{5}{100} + \dfrac{2}{1000} = 257.652$

Write the following in standard form in the space provided.

(a) $1000 + 600 + 30 + 8 + \dfrac{4}{10} + \dfrac{1}{1000}$

=

(b) $6000 + 70 + \dfrac{4}{10} + \dfrac{3}{100} + \dfrac{8}{1000}$

=

(c) $300 + 7 + \dfrac{7}{100}$

=

(d) $80 + 4 + \dfrac{4}{1000}$

=

(e) $3000 + 70 + \dfrac{9}{10} + \dfrac{4}{1000}$

=

(f) $400 + 40 + 9 + \dfrac{4}{10} + \dfrac{6}{100} + \dfrac{7}{1000}$

=

Addition of Decimals

Let's learn how to add the decimals

Remember!
Put a zero before the point if there are no whole numbers.

This strip, which is one unit, is divided into ten equal parts. Let us colour 2 parts and put dots in the other 8 parts. What do you think is the decimal indicated by the coloured parts and by the dotted parts?

I can tell you. The 2 grey parts = 0.2 and the 8 dotted parts = 0.8

2 tenths + 8 tenths = 10 tenths
We can write as,
0.2 + 0.8 = 1.0
We can also write,

$$\begin{array}{r} 0.2 \\ +\ 0.8 \\ \hline 1.0 \end{array}$$

Rules for Addition

> **Remember!**
> Addition of decimals is just like the addition of whole numbers.

> **Remember!**
> To add unlike decimals, add the required number of zeroes at the end and make them like decimals.

> **Remember!**
> Place the decimal points one below the other, both for the addends and the sum.

0.456 + 0.82__   *Add a zero here.*

Look at these examples.

(a) 1.8 + 0.63

O		Tths	Hths
1	•	8	0
0	•	6	3
2	•	4	3

= 2.43

> **Remember!**
> Change unlike decimals to like decimals.

(b) 6.98 + 5.4 + 47.006

H	O		Tths	Hths	Tths
	6	•	9	8	0
	5	•	4	0	0
4	7	•	0	0	6
5	9	•	3	8	6

= 59.386

Notice the position of the decimal points in the above examples.

Exercise 5

Copy vertically and add.

(a) 0.3 + 0.6   (b) 8 + 0.98   (c) 4 + 0.5

(d) 0.48 + 0.09   (e) 0.20 + 0.44   (f) 0.19 + 0.9

(g) 0.41 + 0.49 + 0.61 + 0.52 (h) 0.2 + 0.3 + 0.9 + 0.3 (i) 0.7 + 0.37 + 0.09 + 0.63

(j) 1.53 + 1.25 + 1.06 + 1.20 (k) 9.1 + 11.11 + 777.777 (l) 0.485 + 0.623 + 0.184 + 0.667

Maths Lab Activity 2

Material required

(a) Rectangular cards having decimal numbers   (b) Notebook for each student

Method (Note for the Teacher)

Ask each student to pick any two cards and add their numbers in his/her notebook. Ensure that all of them add correctly. Make their task more challenging in the second round by making them add more than two decimal numbers.

Exercise 6

Match the following by colouring them alike. One has been done for you.

0.006 + 1.098 + 2	23.09 + 1.003 + 456.9	17.091	2.22 + 5.008 + 9	45.909 + 0.33 + 5.678
6.09 + 4 + 7.001	16.228	51.917	3.104	480.993

Subtraction of Decimals

The strip given below, which is equal to one unit, is divided into 10 equal parts. Three portions of the strip are shaded. How many more parts need to be shaded to show one whole?

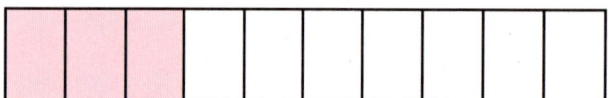

So, 1.0 – 0.3 = 0.7

Rules for Subtraction

> **Remember!**
> Subtraction of decimal numbers is just like subtraction of whole numbers.

> **Remember!**
> Place the decimal points one below the other, both for the numbers and the answer.

> **Remember!**
> To subtract unlike decimals, add zeroes at the end, as required, to make them like decimals.

Look at these examples.

(a) 49.674 – 2.72

T	O		Tths	Hths	THths
4	9	•	6	7	4
	2	•	7	2	0
4	6	•	9	5	4

46.954

(b) 3 – 2.21 (3 is the same as 3.00)

O		Ths	Hths
3	•	0	0
2	•	2	1
0	•	7	9

0.79

> **Remember!**
> The decimal points are placed one below the other.

Exercise 7

(a) Solve this.

```
   6 8 . 5 2 0
 –     1 . 0 2 1
 _____
```

(b) Copy vertically and subtract.

(i) 0.8 – 0.1   (ii) 2.3 – 0.05   (iii) 0.8 – 0.45   (iv) 4.27 – 2.09   (v) 4.8 – 1.9

(vi) 10.6 – 0.12   (vii) 0.9 – 0.75   (viii) 20.4 – 10.39   (ix) 0.45 – 0.08   (x) 181.007 – 16.346

(c) Encircle the correct answer.

  (i) How much is 2.15 subtracted from 4.59? 22.4 2.44 24.4

  (ii) By how much is 4.56 greater than 2.11? 2.45 24.5 25.4

  (iii) What should be subtracted from 2.54 to get 1.10? 14.4 1.44 10.4

  (iv) What should be added to 23.2 to get 40.25? 1.705 170.5 17.05

  (v) By how much should 21.62 be increased to get 50? 28.38 283.8 2.838

  (vi) How much will taking away 1123.51 from 8562.15 give? 743.864 7438.64 7.43864

Multiplication of Decimals

Rules for Multiplication

Rule 1: First, multiply the numbers without considering the decimal point.

Rule 2: Then, count the total number of digits after the point, in both the numbers together.

Rule 3: Put the decimal point in the product so that there are as many digits after the decimal point as you counted.

Look at this example.

5.4×0.12

```
    54
  × 12
  ----
   648
```

There is one digit after the point in the first number and two digits in the second number. So, in total, there are three digits after the decimal point in both the numbers put together. Hence, put the point after three places (starting from the right).

0.648 is your answer.

Remember!
Count the number of places from the right

Exercise 8

After how many places will the decimal point be placed in the answer? (Do not work out the answers.)

Example 3.009×78.1 = after four places.

(a) 3.098×23.89 (b) 123.09×23.9876 (c) 2.9×1.2 (d) 23.111×2.23

Exercise 9

(a) Multiply the following. Write the answer as decimal. One has been done for you.

(i) 0.8×0.2

$$\begin{array}{r} 0.8 \\ \times\ 0.2 \\ \hline 16 \end{array}$$

$= 0.16$

(ii) 0.7×0.4

(iii) 1.5×0.6

(iv) 14.8×0.2

(v) 19.3×0.8

(vi) 36.6×0.4

(vii) 1.51×4.2

(viii) 3.16×2.31

(ix) 0.83×5.5515

(b) Change to fractions first and then multiply. Write the answer as decimal. One has been done for you.

(i) 1.5×0.003

$$\frac{15}{10} \times \frac{3}{1000}$$

$$\frac{15 \times 3}{10000} = \frac{45}{10000}$$

$= 0.0045$

(ii) 0.555×5.5

(iii) 13.04×19.41

(iv) 14.04×12.4

(v) 82.8×1.623

(vi) 63.4×0.00053

(vii) 15.8×66.8

(viii) 99.9×0.00011

(ix) 54.1×63.2

Word Attack

(a) Find the product of 12121.2 and 0.0212.

(b) Find out 0.08 of 8800 kg.

(c) A school van covers a distance of 34.25 km to pick students from their homes in a day. What distance will it cover in 66 days?

(d) A jeans manufacturing company got an order to stitch 356 pairs of jeans. Each pair of jeans requires 2.856 m of cloth. How much cloth is required to make 356 such pairs?

Multiplying a Decimal by 10, 100 and 1000

Look at these.

5.23 × 10 = 52.30 = 52.3
6.35 × 100 = 635.00 = 635
25.9 × 100 = 2590.0 = 2590
0.611 × 1000 = 611.000 = 611

Remember!
To multiply a decimal by 10, move the decimal point one place to the right.

Remember!
To multiply a decimal by 100, move the decimal point two places to the right.

Ha! Ha! ...
Now I understand!
To multiply by 1000, move the decimal point three places to the right.

Exercise 10

Find the product.

(a) 0.6 × 10

(b) 0.56 × 10

(c) 0.889 × 10

(d) 3.36 × 10

(e) 0.58 × 100

(f) 0.9 × 100

(g) 0.866 × 100   (h) 25.896 × 100   (i) 62.1 × 1000

(j) 38.66 × 1000   (k) 9.1235 × 1000   (l) 0.21 × 1000

Division of Decimals

Rules for Division

Rule 1: You cannot divide by a decimal number or fraction. So, first convert the divisor into a whole number.

Rule 2: Place the decimal point in the quotient directly above the decimal point in the dividend.

Rule 3: In the absence of a whole number in the dividend, place a zero in the quotient.

Look at this example.

Method 1

$0.8 \div 2$

$$\begin{array}{r} 0.4 \\ 2\overline{)0.8} \\ \underline{0} \\ 8 \\ \underline{8} \\ 0 \end{array}$$

(Since there is no whole number in the dividend, zero is placed in the quotient in its place.)

Method 2

$0.8 \div 2$

$$\frac{8}{10} \div \frac{2}{1} = \frac{8}{10} \times \frac{1}{2} = \frac{8}{20} = \frac{4}{10} = 0.4$$

Let us take another example.

Method 1

0.064 ÷ 8

```
       0.008
    ┌────────
  8 ) 0.064
       0
       ───
       064
        64
       ───
         0
```

→ '0' is placed in the quotient since there is no whole number in the dividend.
→ As 6 < 8, place a zero in the quotient and bring down the next digit (4) to make it 64.

> **Remember!**
> When you cross a decimal point in the dividend, place a point in the quotient also.

Method 2

0.064 ÷ 8

$= \dfrac{64}{1000} \div \dfrac{8}{1}$

$= \dfrac{64}{1000} \times \dfrac{1}{8} = \dfrac{64}{8000} = \dfrac{8}{1000} = 0.008$

Exercise 11

Find the quotient.

(a) 0.8 ÷ 4 (b) 0.75 ÷ 5 (c) 12.6 ÷ 9

(d) 0.36 ÷ 2 (e) 2.965 ÷ 5 (f) 0.0021 ÷ 7

(g) $0.072 \div 8$ (h) $43.65 \div 50$ (i) $18.675 \div 15$

Division by a Decimal

To divide by a decimal, you have to convert the divisor into a whole number.

Look at the example.

Example 1 $0.645 \div 0.5$

$$= \frac{0.645}{0.5} = \frac{0.645 \times 10}{0.5 \times 10}$$

> **Remember!**
> To convert the divisor into a whole number,
> × 10 if there is one digit after the point
> × 100 if there are two digits after the point
> × 1000 if there are three digits after the point
> Multiply the numerator also to retain the value.

We multiply the numerator and denominator by 10 to make the divisor a whole number.

$$= \frac{6.45}{5} =$$

```
      1.29
  5) 6.45
     5
     ---
     14
     10
     ---
      45
      45
     ---
       0
```

Let us take another example.

Example 2 $1.6 \div 0.08$

$$= \frac{1.6}{0.08} = \frac{1.6 \times 100}{0.08 \times 100}$$

(Multiply the denominator by 100 to change it into a whole number. Multiply the numerator also by 100 in order to keep the value unchanged.)

$$= \frac{160.0}{8} = 20$$

```
     20
  8) 160
     160
     ---
       0
```

Exercise 12

Divide the following.

(a) 2.12 ÷ 5.3

(b) 0.004 ÷ 0.2

(c) 0.52 ÷ 0.013

(d) 18.675 ÷ 1.5

(e) 0.435 ÷ 0.5

(f) 0.0552 ÷ 0.6

(g) 35.052 ÷ 2.3

(h) 0.81 ÷ 0.9

(i) 0.3874 ÷ 0.2

Division by 10, 100 and 1000

Look at these examples.

15.73 ÷ 10 = 1.573

15.73 ÷ 100 = 0.1573

15.73 ÷ 1000 = 0.01573

Dividing by 10 moves the decimal point one place to the left in the answer.

Dividing by 100 moves the decimal point two places to the left in the answer.

Dividing by 1000 moves the decimal point three places to the left in the answer.

> **Observe the changes in the place of the decimal.**

> **Remember!**
> When multiplying by 10, move decimal point to the right.
> When dividing by 10, move decimal point to the left.

Exercise 13

Divide the following.

(a) 601.43 ÷ 10   (b) 52.56 ÷ 10   (c) 6.899 ÷ 10

(d) 16.111 ÷ 100   (e) 222.56 ÷ 100   (f) 1.4236 ÷ 100

(g) 256.5 ÷ 1000   (h) 565.65 ÷ 1000   (i) 0.3331 ÷ 1000

Exercise 14

(a) Multiply the number on the chimney by the numbers given on the windows and write the answers in the space provided.

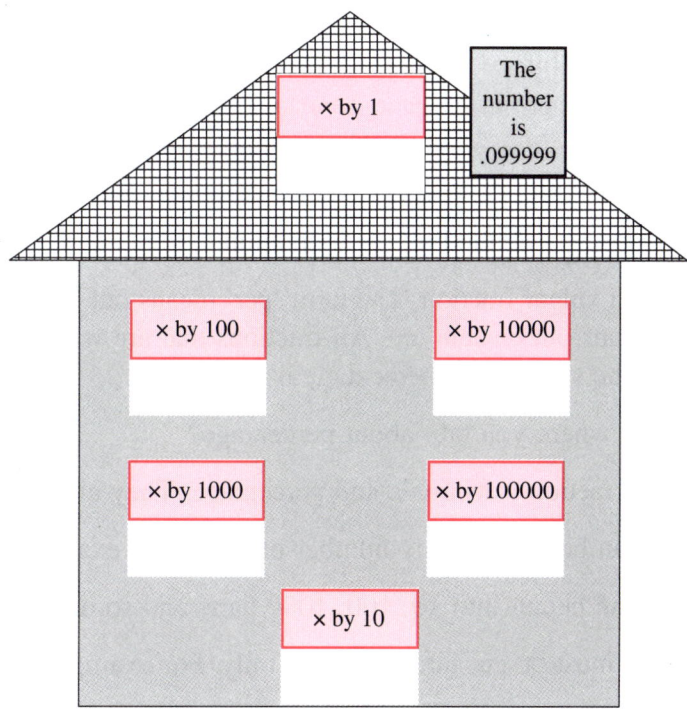

(b) Divide the number on the chimney by the numbers given on the windows and write the answers in the space provided.

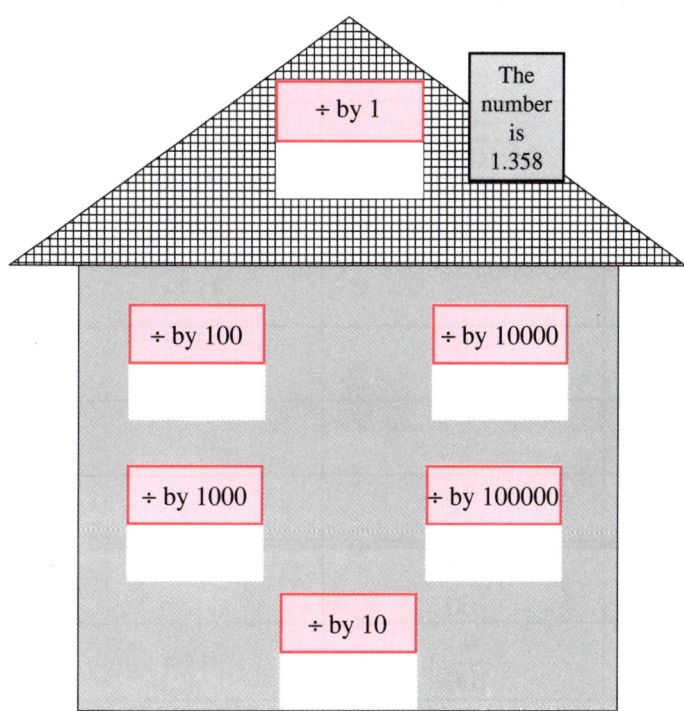

Chapter 9

Percentage

> **You know...**
> - there is comparison all around us
> - we require a standard to compare in order to be accurate.

A fraction in the form 0.75 is called a *decimal* fraction.

An equivalent fraction in the form $\frac{3}{4}$ is called a *vulgar* fraction.

Percentages are ratios written as a vulgar fraction. The term 'per' means out of and 'cent' means hundred. So, the word *percentage* actually means *out of hundred*. All fractions that are written with a denominator of 100 can be written as percentages. The symbol for percentage is %.

Can you think of three activities where you talk about percentage?

There is a relationship between fractions, decimals and percentage. They all show part of a whole.

(a) In fractions, the whole can be cut into any number of parts. For example, $\frac{7}{19}$.

(b) In decimals, the whole can be cut into 10, 100, 1000 parts and so on. For example, 0.50.

(c) In percentage, the whole must be cut into 100 parts only. For example, 50%.

Exercise 1

Complete the following table.

Per cent	Fraction	Decimal
25%		0.25
40%	$\frac{40}{100}$	
	$\frac{10}{100}$	0.1
33%		0.33
75%	$\frac{75}{100}$	
1%		0.01
20%	$\frac{20}{100}$	
14%	$\frac{14}{100}$	
	$\frac{4}{100}$	0.04

Diagrams can also be used to represent percentage.

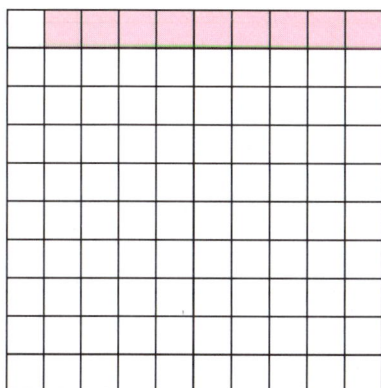

This diagram has been divided into 100 parts and 9 parts out of 100 are coloured. A fraction that has 100 as its denominator is called a percentage. So this can be expressed as 9% or called 9 per cent. The number of parts not coloured is 91 out of 100. This can be expressed as 91% or called 91 per cent.

9%   91%

Exercise 2

Express both the shaded and not shaded parts as percentages.

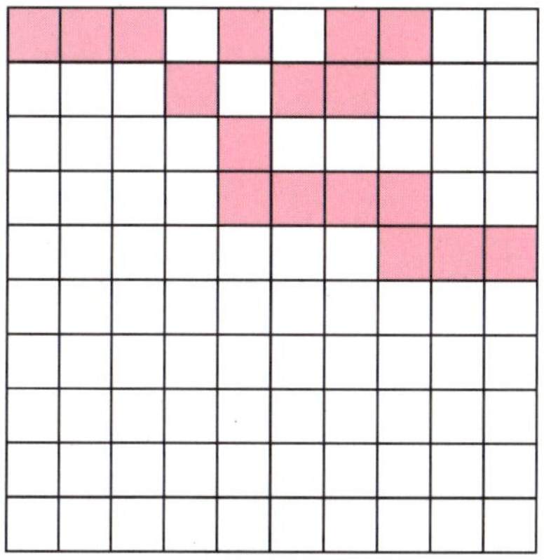

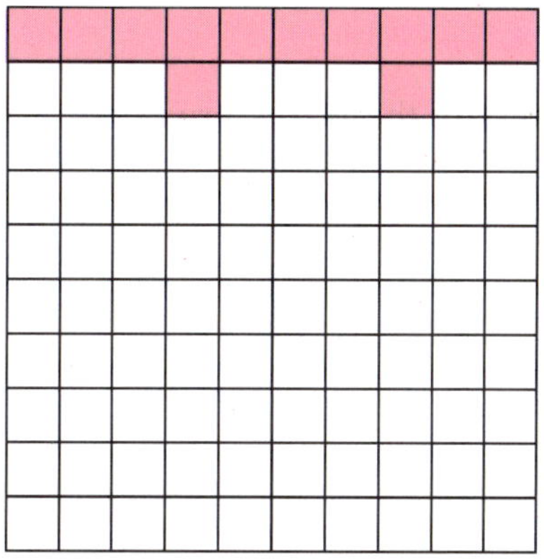

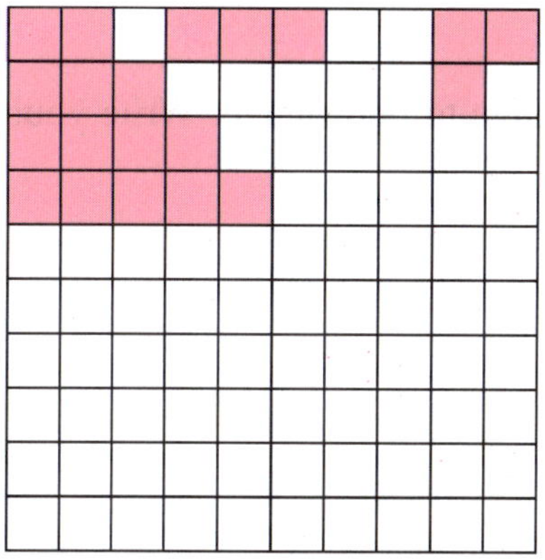

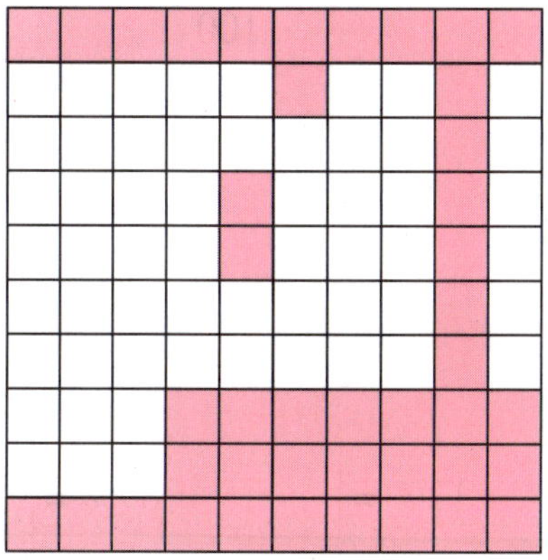

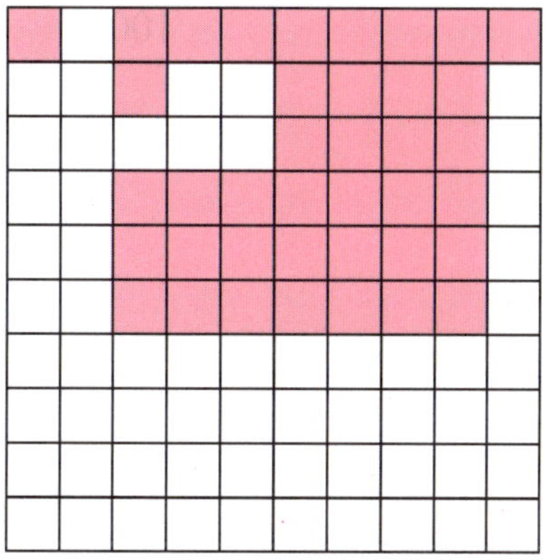

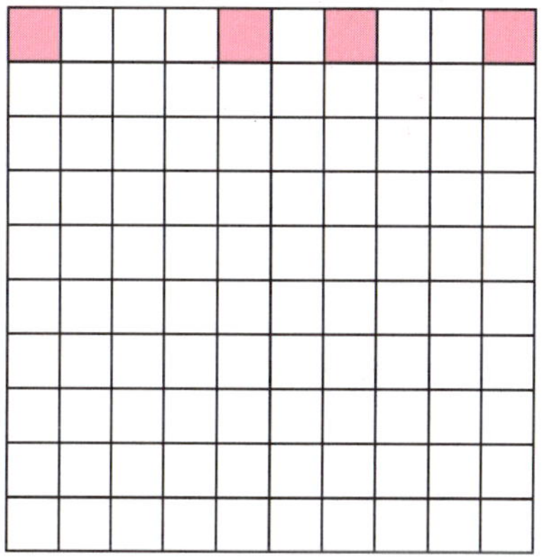

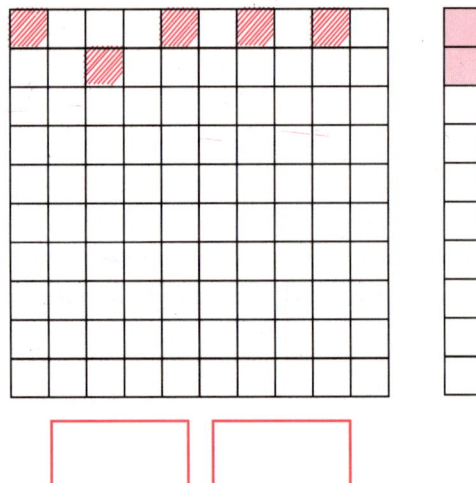 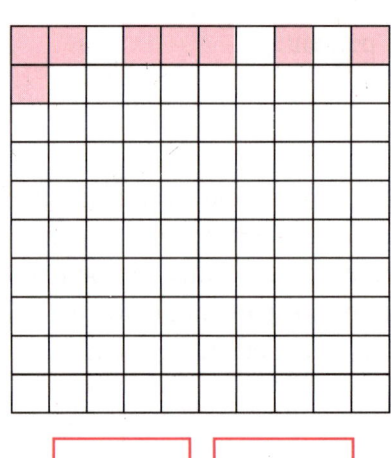 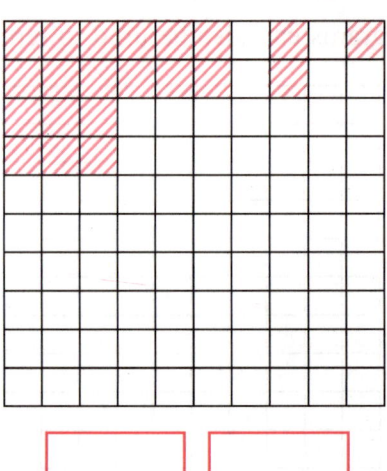

Exercise 3

Change to percentage. Write your answers in the boxes provided.

(a) $\frac{2}{100}$ = ☐   (b) $\frac{6}{100}$ = ☐   (c) $\frac{12}{100}$ = ☐   (d) $\frac{78}{100}$ = ☐

(e) $\frac{50}{100}$ = ☐   (f) $\frac{99}{100}$ = ☐   (g) $\frac{34}{100}$ = ☐   (h) $\frac{80}{100}$ = ☐

(i) $\frac{15}{100}$ = ☐   (j) $\frac{82}{100}$ = ☐   (k) $\frac{67}{100}$ = ☐   (l) $\frac{33}{100}$ = ☐

Exercise 4

Change to fractions.

(a) 34% = ☐   (b) 45% = ☐   (c) 67% = ☐   (d) 58% = ☐   (e) 12% = ☐   (f) 89% = ☐

(g) 11% = ☐   (h) 99% = ☐   (i) 27% = ☐   (j) 78% = ☐   (k) 19% = ☐   (l) 68% = ☐

You must have often heard people using percentages in their conversation, but wondered what they meant. Here are some fractions also expressed as percentages. They will help you understand percentages better.

- 50% = 1/2
- 25% = 1/4
- 75% = 3/4
- 100% = 1
- 33 1/3% = 1/3
- 66 2/3% = 2/3
- 20% = 1/5
- 0.01 = 1%
- 10% = 1/10
- 5% = 1/20
- 1% = 1/100
- 1.0 = 100%
- 0.75 = 75%
- 0.50 = 50%
- 0.25 = 25%

Exercise 5

Match the two columns by colouring like expressions with the same colour.

10% of the students were absent today.	$\frac{3}{4}$
50% of my homework is done.	$\frac{1}{20}$
25% of the cake was eaten by Rakesh alone.	$\frac{1}{3}$
Radhika scored 75% in her Maths test yesterday.	$\frac{2}{3}$
Not even 1% of the students missed the concert.	1
Only 5% of the participants were able to complete the race.	$\frac{1}{5}$
Sam has completed reading $33\frac{1}{3}$% of the story.	$\frac{1}{100}$
Around 20% of the girls have joined the girl guides.	$\frac{1}{2}$
Sheija invited $66\frac{2}{3}$% of her class for the party.	$\frac{1}{10}$
There was 100% attendance in the school today.	$\frac{1}{4}$

Only a fraction with a denominator of 100 can be converted to a percentage. So, first you should change the denominator of the given fraction to 100. Remember, when you multiply the denominator with its reciprocal, you have to do the same to the numerator also, so that the value of the fraction does not change.

Example $\dfrac{2}{5}$

Is it possible to change 5 to 100? How?

Multiply 2 by 20 and 5 by 20 to get the new fraction.

$\dfrac{2 \times 20}{5 \times 20} = \dfrac{40}{100}$ This means 40%.   Hence, $\dfrac{2}{5} = 40\%$

Exercise 6

Now change the following fractions to percentages.

(a) $\dfrac{3}{5}$ (b) $\dfrac{5}{10}$ (c) $\dfrac{7}{20}$

(d) $\dfrac{8}{25}$ (e) $\dfrac{3}{50}$ (f) $\dfrac{3}{4}$

Converting a Mixed Number into Percentage

Mixed numbers can be converted into improper fractions and then multiplied by a suitable fraction whose value should always remain one. Once the denominator becomes 100, it can be expressed as percentage.

$$2\dfrac{1}{4} = \dfrac{9}{4} \times \dfrac{25}{25} = \dfrac{225}{100} = 225\%$$

Exercise 7

Now convert the following to percentage.

(a) $3\dfrac{1}{2}$ (b) $4\dfrac{6}{20}$ (c) $4\dfrac{1}{5}$

(d) $2\dfrac{4}{25}$ (e) $3\dfrac{1}{10}$ (f) $7\dfrac{1}{4}$

Converting a Decimal into Percentage

Example 0.8

You know that 0.8 = 8/10. Here again, you have to change the denominator to 100, if it is not already 100, and then write it as a percentage. So, the expression becomes 80/100 = 80%.

Exercise 8

Now solve the following.

(a) 0.9   (b) 0.15   (c) 0.2

(d) 0.25   (e) 0.3   (f) 0.45

It is also possible to find the percentage of a number.

Example

$$25\% \text{ of } 60$$

$$= \frac{25}{100} \text{ of } 60 = \frac{\overset{1}{\cancel{25}}}{\underset{4}{\cancel{100}}} \times 60 = \frac{60}{4} = 15 \quad \text{So, } 25\% \text{ of } 60 = 15.$$

Exercise 9

Now solve the following. Use the space provided.

(a) 10% of 80 (b) 30% of 120 (c) 35% of 240

(d) 40% of 160 (e) 22% of 1000 (f) 5% of 800

(g) 18% of 3600 (h) 50% of 1750 (i) 16% of 6400

Converting a Fraction into Percentage

Example

Find what percentage is 10 out of 20.

Method 1

$$\frac{10}{20} = \boxed{}$$

To find the percentage, we need to make the denominator 100.

So, 20 × 5 gives 100 and 10 × 5 will give 50. So, 10/20 is 50/100 = 50%.

Method 2

We can also use the unitary method to find the percentage of a fraction.

The given fraction is (10 out of 20). This is like Rs. 10 for 20 mangoes.

We need to find out how much it is out of 100. (That is, how much it is for 100 mangoes.)

Cost of 20 = 10

Cost of 100 = $\frac{10}{20} \times 100 = \frac{1000}{20} = 50$.   (It is 50 per 100 or 50%)

Method 3

You can apply the ratio method also to find the percentage of a fraction.

$$10 : 20 :: x : 100 \Rightarrow 20x = 1000$$

$$x = \frac{1000}{20} = 50\%$$

Exercise 10

Find what percentage are the following.

(a) 12 out of 40

(b) 15 out of 750

(c) 20 out of 880

(d) 75 out of 950

(e) 6 out of 360

(f) 4 out of 110

Word Attack

(a) There are 360 students in a school. 30% of them are girls and the rest are boys. What is the percentage of boys? Also, find how many girls and boys are there in the school?

(b) Raghu earned Rs. 6500 per month. He saved 30% of his salary every month. What is the amount he saved every month and how much did he spend in terms of rupees?

(c) There are 40 students in a class. In a Geography test, 15% of the students scored marks above 80, 10% of the students scored between 60 and 80 and the rest scored below 60. How many students scored marks below 60? Also, find their percentage.

(d) 90 out of the 600 students, who appeared in a science talent test, failed. What is the number of such students in terms of percentage? How many students passed the test?

(e) Shyam sat for an aptitude test to join an engineering course. He was able to answer 14 questions out of 20. What percentage is that? What is the percentage of the questions he could not answer?

(f) In a village, 32% of the population were women, 12% were children and the rest were men. If the total population of the village was 5200, find out the number of men, women and children.

Exercise 11

Correct the mistakes in the following sentences and rewrite.

(a) The word 'cent' means thousand. _____

(b) $\frac{30}{100}$ is the same as 3%. _____

(c) Percentage is always calculated out of 10. _____

(d) $\frac{7}{10}$ is the same as 7%. _____

(e) While percentages can be expressed as fractions, they cannot be expressed as decimals.
_____

(f) ÷ is the symbol for percentage. _____

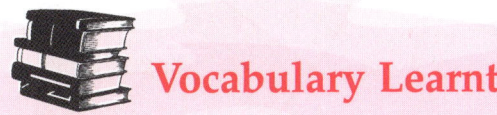

Vocabulary Learnt

per cent   express   relationship
         convert   symbol
vulgar   accurate

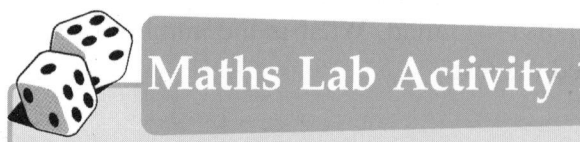

Maths Lab Activity 1

Materials required

(a) A table for each student with information about different languages spoken by different percentage of people in India

(b) Crayons

Method (Note for the Teacher)

Ask all the students to make a pie chart and colour the percentage of different languages spoken in India on the pie chart.

(a)	English	15%	(b)	Hindi	27%
(c)	Punjabi	11%	(d)	Marathi	8%
(e)	Gujarati	6%	(f)	Tamil	7%
(g)	Bengali	9%	(h)	Telugu	4%
(i)	Kannada	3%	(j)	Other languages	10%

If the total population is 1,03,52,46,900, ask them to find the number of people speaking each of the languages listed above and write the numbers in the respective parts on the pie chart.

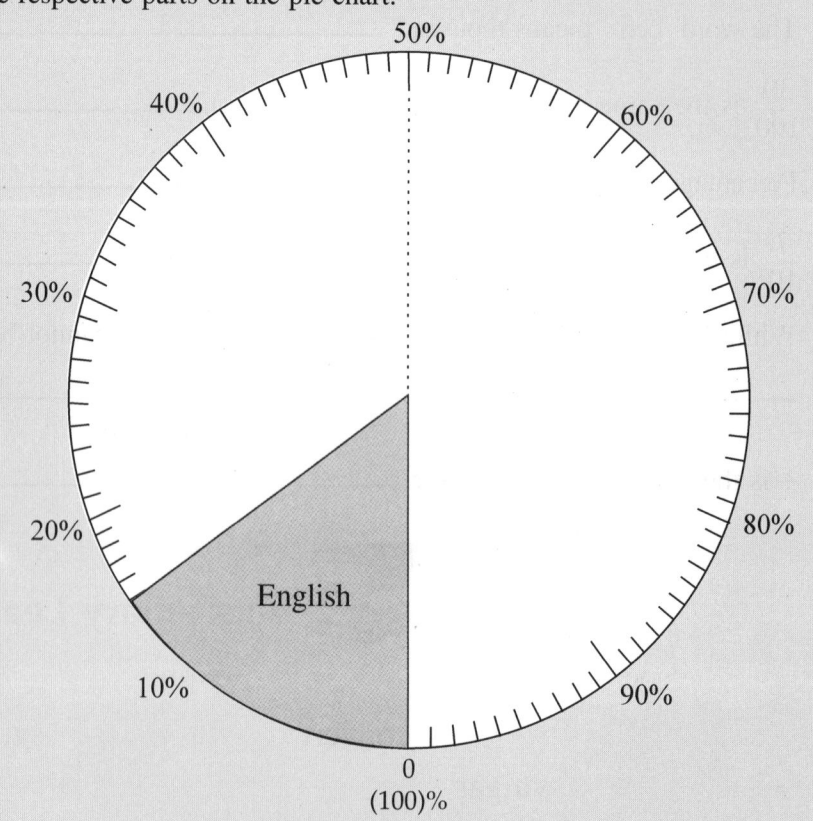

Chapter 10 — Ratio and Proportion

> **You know...**
> - how to compare two or more numbers
> - that for comparison of two or more things, they must be of similar value, strength or quantity.

Ratio is all about comparing quantities. 'X' has 2 bananas and 'Y' has 3 apples. The ratio of the fruits they have is 2 : 3 and it is read as 2 is to 3. If they had 4 bananas and 2 apples, then it could be read as 4 : 2. This could also be expressed in the ratio 2 : 1 by reducing them to their lowest term. Similarly, if there are 2 apples for 4 bananas, there would be 1 apple for 2 bananas. If 'X' had 2 bananas and 'Y' had 3 apples, the ratio would still be 2 : 3. A ratio can be cancelled in the same way as fractions, in order to reduce it to its lowest term. Ratio can also be expressed as a fraction.

Example

20 : 10 can also be written as $\frac{20}{10}$. (The denominator here does not mean that there are only that many parts in the number.)

Similarly, 10 : 20 can be written as $\frac{10}{20}$.

Exercise 1

Answer the questions given below.

A shopkeeper gives a boy a free pencil for every three books he buys.

(a) What is the ratio of pencils to books?

(b) If the boy buys 6 books, how many pencils will he get?
What will be the ratio of books to pencils?

(c) If he buys 12 books, how many pencils would he get?

(d) If he gets 6 pencils, how many books would he have bought?

(e) How many books must he buy to get 10 pencils?
Write the ratio for this situation.

Order of Numbers in a Ratio

The order in which you write the numbers should always coincide with the order in which the information is given.

For example, you have some oranges and bananas and if their ratio is 3 : 1, it means you have 3 oranges for every one banana. You cannot write it as 1 : 3 because that would mean that for every orange you have 3 bananas. So, the order of numbers is very important in ratio.

Exercise 2

Express the following as a ratio.

(a) 10 girls to 15 boys

(b) 15 minutes to 75 minutes

(c) 15 men to 45 women

(d) 16 years to 80 years

There are no units in ratio; it is just a comparison of numbers and not the actual quantities. But you have to remember that when two quantities are compared, they must be in the same unit. For example, if you want to compare 75 p with 2 rupees, convert the rupees also into paise before writing the ratio. You cannot write it as 75 : 2. 2 rupees = 200 paise, so the ratio is 75 : 200, which will become 3 : 8 in its lowest term.

Exercise 3

Convert to the same unit and write the ratio for the following.

(a) 3 hours to 24 minutes

(b) 5 days to 2 weeks

(c) 1 m to 20 cm

(d) 350 g to 1 ½ kg

(e) 9 months to 3 years

(f) 200 m to 5 km

Ratios do not have fractions in them.

Example

$2\frac{1}{2}$: 2 cannot be compared because one term is a fraction while the other is a whole number. So, we need to convert the one with a fraction into a whole number. Here, $2\frac{1}{2}$ multiplied by 2 will make it 5. The other term also needs to be multiplied by 2 (2 × 2 = 4) in order to keep the ratio unchanged. So the ratio is 5 : 4.

Exercise 4

Convert the following ratios to like terms and reduce wherever possible.

(a) $1\frac{1}{4} : 5$

(b) $\frac{4}{5} : 6$

(c) $3\frac{1}{2} : 10$

(d) $2\frac{3}{4} : 9$

(e) $1\frac{1}{3} : 12$

(f) $3\frac{1}{2} : 21$

Comparing Ratios

To compare two fractions, you always change them to like fractions, where the two fractions will have the same denominators. Similarly, when you want to compare two ratios, you can express them as fractions first and then do just what you would do to compare fractions.

Example 1 : 2 and 3 : 5

Step 1: Write both the ratios as fractions $1 : 2 = \frac{1}{2}$ and $3 : 5 = \frac{3}{5}$

Step 2: Find the L.C.M. for the two denominators. Here it is 10.

Step 3: $\frac{1}{2}$ is equal to $\frac{5}{10}$ and $\frac{3}{5}$ is equal to $\frac{6}{10}$. So $\frac{6}{10}$ is greater than $\frac{5}{10}$.

Therefore 3 : 5 > 1 : 2.

Exercise 5

Compare the following ratios.

(a) 5 : 8 and 6 : 9

(b) 1 : 3 and 4 : 5

(c) 6 : 7 and 5 : 8

(d) 5 : 10 and 8 : 14

(e) 2 : 11 and 12 : 21

(f) 3 : 5 and 5 : 3

Proportion

When two ratios represent equal quantities, they are said to be in proportion. Each set of ratio may have different quantities, but their proportion may be the same.

For example, 2 : 5 and 4 : 10 are said to be in proportion because, when you reduce 4 : 10, it becomes 2 : 5. The two end terms are called the extremes and the two inner terms are called the means. ': :' is the symbol used for proportion. It means 'is in proportion to'.

Another way of finding out whether the two ratios are in proportion is to multiply the two extremes together and the two means together. If their products are equal, the two ratios are said to be in proportion.

Example

3 : 9 : : 9 : 27. To prove this, you can multiply the two extremes (3 × 27 = 81) and the two means (9 × 9 = 81).

Exercise 6

Fill in the blanks to make the ratios proportionate.

(a) 3 : 5 : : 15 : ☐   (b) 6 : 10 : : 36 : ☐   (c) 4 : ☐ : : 16 : 24

(d) ☐ : 11 : : 46 : 22   (e) ☐ : 10 : : 60 : 100   (f) 3 : 2 : : ☐ : 16

Exercise 7

Find out whether the following ratios are in proportion.

Use a ✓ to say Yes and a ✗ to say No.

(a) 3 : 16 : : 9 : 18 ☐   (b) 5 : 20 : : 10 : 30 ☐   (c) 49 : 56 : : 8 : 9 ☐

(d) 1 : 2 : : 4 : 8 ☐   (e) 2 : 12 : : 4 : 15 ☐   (f) 18 : 72 : : 25 : 100 ☐

Word Attack

(a) There are 180 boys and 240 girls in the primary section of the school. Find the ratio of boys to girls and express this in its lowest term.

(b) There are 25 mangoes for every 75 bananas in a fruit shop. Write the ratio of the mangoes to the bananas in its lowest term.

(c) The ratio of men and women in a tiny village is 2 : 3. If there are 612 men, how many women are there?

(d) The ratio between the numbers for the distance travelled and the quantity of petrol consumed is 32 : 2. If the distance travelled is 480 km, how much petrol has been used?

(e) The length and breadth of an assembly hall are in the ratio 5 : 3. If the length of the assembly hall is 15 m, what will be its breadth?

(f) A batsman hit 3 fours for every six that he hit. If he hit 4 sixes, how many fours did he hit?

(g) The ratio of Tina's age to her father's age is 1 : 4. If her father's age is 36, what is her age?

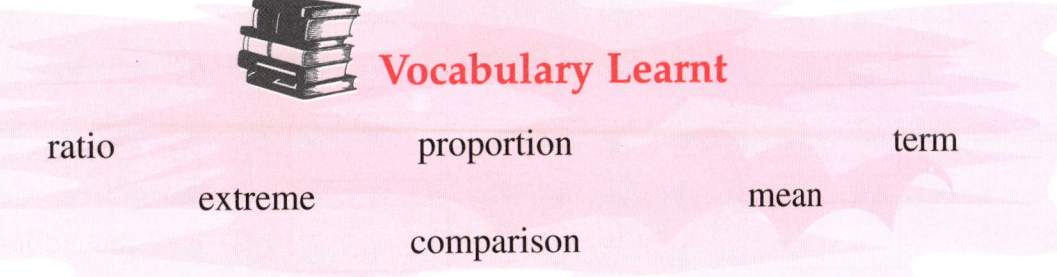

Vocabulary Learnt

ratio　　　　　　　proportion　　　　　　　term
　　　extreme　　　　　　　　　mean
　　　　　　comparison

Maths Lab Activity 1

Materials required

(a) A worksheet as shown below for every student (b) Pencil

Method (Note for the Teacher)

Give each student a worksheet. Ask the students to observe the pictures carefully and find the ratios for the list given below.

Example

Ratio of butterflies to flowers = 5 : 6. Since this ratio cannot be reduced further, leave it like that.

(a) dogs : ducks ☐ (b) clouds : flowers ☐ (c) hats : trees ☐

(d) squirrels : girls ☐ (e) hats : girls ☐ (f) girls : flowers ☐

(g) dogs : trees ☐ (h) girls : dogs ☐ (i) hats : butterflies ☐

Chapter 11 Profit and Loss

> **You know…**
> - the meaning of buying and selling
> - money transactions can involve a gain or a loss
> - the operation used for finding loss or gain.

What is profit?

Example 1

Mr Rishi, an electrical appliances shop owner, bought a new model of television set for Rs. 60,000. Since it was very new to the market, he was able to sell it to a customer for Rs. 1,00,000.

The money Mr Rishi paid to buy the television set is called the **cost price**.

The money Mr Rishi received by selling the television is the **selling price**.

Did he get any extra money?

Yes, he received Rs. 40,000 more than what he spent. So, that is his gain.

> **Remember!**
> The extra amount of money over the cost price is called profit or gain.

Example 2

> Gain or Profit = Selling Price (S.P.) − Cost Price (C.P.)

Mr Prabhu, who also owns an electrical goods shop, tried to sell the same television set. But he was not so lucky to get a customer. Finally, he sold it for Rs. 50,000. This amount is also called the selling price.

Did he get any extra money? No, he did not. In fact, he got Rs. 10,000 less than the cost price. So, there is a loss.

Exercise 1

> Loss = Cost Price (C.P.) − Selling Price (S.P.)

Example

C.P. = Rs. 8000; S.P. = Rs. 10,000.

So, profit = S.P. − C.P. = 10,000 − 8000 = Rs. 2000

Now, find the profit for the following values of C.P. and S.P.

(a) C.P. = Rs. 855; S.P. = Rs. 955

(b) C.P. = Rs. 95,000; S.P. = Rs. 1,20,000

(c) C.P. = Rs. 17,850; S.P. = Rs. 25,105

(d) C.P. = Rs. 1,24,500; S.P. = Rs. 1,49,320

Exercise 2

Example

$$\text{C.P.} = \text{Rs. } 12{,}000; \quad \text{S.P.} = \text{Rs. } 10{,}000$$

$$\text{So loss} = \text{C.P.} - \text{S.P.} = 12{,}000 - 10{,}000 = \text{Rs. } 2000$$

Now, find the loss for the following values of C.P. and S.P.

(a) C.P. = Rs. 3450; S.P. = Rs. 2250

(b) C.P. = Rs. 9850; S.P. = Rs. 6745

(c) C.P. = Rs. 455; S.P. = Rs. 300

(d) C.P. = Rs. 588; S.P. = Rs. 410

Exercise 3

Find the profit or loss and its amount.

Items	Cost Price (C.P.)	Selling Price (S.P.)	Profit/Loss	Profit/Loss in Rupees
Mixer grinder	Rs. 5000	Rs. 6000	Profit	Profit = S.P. – C.P. = 6000 – 5000 = Rs. 1000
Oven	Rs. 7500	Rs. 5200		
Radio	Rs. 800	Rs. 1100		
Television	Rs. 12,000	Rs. 15,000		
Electric heater	Rs. 6150	Rs. 7820		

Exercise 4

Fill in the missing quantities.

Items	Cost Price (C.P.)	Selling Price (S.P.)	Profit/Loss	Amount of profit or loss
Water bottle	Rs. 85	Rs. 100	Profit	
School bag		Rs. 500	Profit	Rs. 150
Tiffin career	Rs. 285	Rs. 225	Loss	
Air conditioner	Rs. 32,000		Profit	Rs. 10,000
Stroller bag		Rs. 4200	profit	Rs. 1000

Percentage of Profit or Loss

The loss or gain on an item can also be expressed as a percentage.

Example Rita had a beautiful dress tailored for Rs. 500 at her shop. She sold it for Rs. 800. She made a profit of Rs. 300 and was very happy.

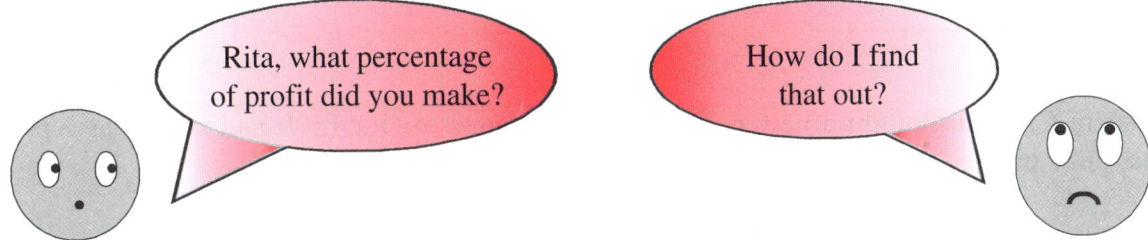

Look at this. Cost Price = Rs. 500

Selling Price = Rs. 800   So, profit = Rs. 800 – Rs. 500 = Rs. 300.

The profit on Rs. 500 is 300.

The profit on Rs. 100 will be = $\dfrac{\cancel{300}^{60}}{\cancel{500}_{1}} \times \cancel{100}$ (Simplify the fraction wherever possible.)

So, percentage of profit = 60 or 60%

| Percentage of Profit = $\dfrac{\text{Profit} \times 100}{\text{Cost Price}}$ | Percentage of Loss = $\dfrac{\text{Loss} \times 100}{\text{Cost Price}}$ |

Exercise 5

Now solve the following table.

Cost Price	Selling Price	Profit/Loss	Find Profit/Loss in Rupees	% of Profit/Loss
Rs. 3000	Rs. 3600	Profit	= S.P. – C.P. = 3600 – 3000 = 600	= $\dfrac{600}{\cancel{3000}}\times\cancel{100}$ = 20%
Rs. 2500	Rs. 3100			
Rs. 1500	Rs. 1725			
Rs. 190	Rs. 60			
Rs. 600	Rs. 570			

Converting Profit/Loss per cent to Rupees

If the profit/loss per cent is given, use the following formulae to calculate profit and loss respectively.

$$\text{Profit} = \frac{\text{Profit \%} \times \text{C.P.}}{100} \qquad \text{Loss} = \frac{\text{Loss \%} \times \text{C.P.}}{100}$$

Example

A shop owner in Chennai bought a new model of room heater for Rs. 1500 and sold it at a profit of 25%. At what price did he sell the product?

Profit amount = 25% of C.P.   Or, $\dfrac{25 \times 1500}{100}$ = Rs. 375.00

S.P. = C.P. + Profit = 1500 + 375 = Rs. 1875.00

Word Attack

(a) A fruit seller bought 100 pineapples for Rs. 900 and made a profit of 35%. Find the selling price of the 100 pineapples.

(b) Ramya bought a bicycle for Rs. 6540 and sold it after 2 years at a loss of 20%. What is the loss incurred by her?

(c) A van was bought for Rs. 3,24,910 and sold for Rs. 2,92,419. Find out the profit or loss of the van owner and find the percentage also.

(d) Raju bought a house for Rs. 10 lakhs and spent Rs. 2 lakhs on woodwork and interior decoration. After 2 years, he sold the house for Rs. 18 lakhs. Find his profit and profit percentage.

(e) A man bought a video camera from Singapore for Rs. 85,500. After his return to India, he sold it to his friend at a gain of 15%. What is the selling price?

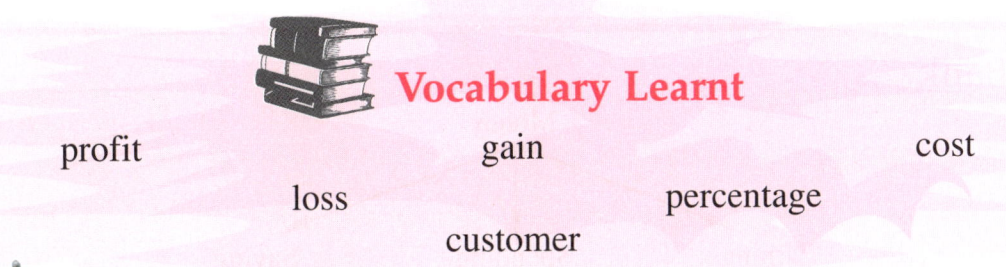

Vocabulary Learnt

profit   gain   cost
   loss   percentage
       customer

Maths Lab Activity 1

Materials required

(a) A picture card for each student   (b) Paper   (c) Pencil

Method (Note for the Teacher)

Give each student a card and ask them to write a word problem involving profit or loss, using the picture as part of the word problem. Ask them to read aloud their word problems to see if they have understood the concept correctly. They can exchange the cards and write more problems using different situations. Pictures of some objects are given below.

Chapter 12 — Simple Interest

> **You know...**
> - we all need money
> - why we need money.

Role of a Bank

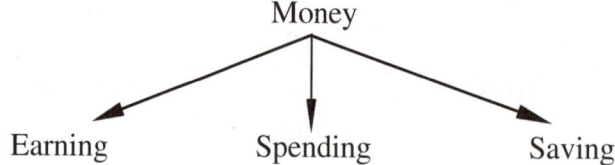

How do your parents earn?

All of us have to do some work to earn money. With the money earned, we take care of all our needs. So, we spend the money. But it is very important to save money. Can you think of two reasons why we should save money?

(a) _____

(b) _____

We must have money in reserve for any future expenses that may come up suddenly or to buy things that we normally do not budget for every month. So, how do we save? How do we protect the money we save?

Here, the **bank** comes to our rescue.

A bank is an organisation which keeps your money safe. At the end of a fixed period, which has been agreed upon (by you and the bank), it returns you more money than the amount you deposited. This extra money is called **interest**. Do you know why the bank gives interest?

The bank pays interest for allowing the bank to lend your money to others, mostly businessmen, to improve their business. While the bank gives you interest for saving money, it collects more interest from the person to whom it lends your money.

Look at this chart and you will know how it works.

Let us look at some examples.

(a) Mr Prakash deposited Rs. 5000.00 in the bank for a period of 1 year. When the bank returned his money, he got Rs. 5500.00. This means, he got Rs. 500.00 more. This is called the 'interest' on his deposit.

(b) The City National Bank lent Rs. 25,000.00 for 1 year to Mr Raju to start a small business. After the completion of one year, Mr Raju returned Rs 30,000.00 to the bank. This means the bank got an interest of Rs. 5000.00 from Mr Raju for lending him money for his business.

The Reserve Bank of India, a government bank, is the only authorised organisation to mint/print money for circulation. It controls all the banks of India.

Principal, Amount and Interest

The money you deposit in a bank is called the 'principal'.

The extra money returned to you by the bank is called the 'interest'.

The total money returned by the bank is called the 'amount'.

Amount A = P + I

Given below are some formulae. Study them carefully. In the houses given below, pink colour stands for amount (A), white for principal (P) and grey for interest (I).

To find the amount, which is always the largest of the three: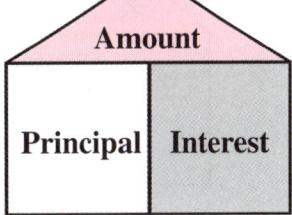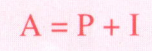

A = P + I

To find the interest, when the amount and principal are given: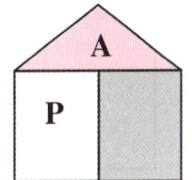

I = A − P

To find the principal, when the amount and interest are given: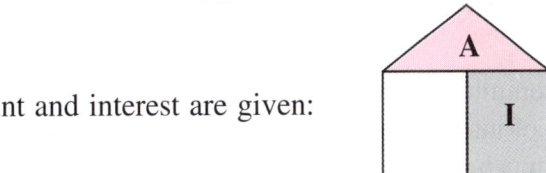

P = A − I

Exercise 1

Fill in the blank boxes by using the given colour code. One has been done for you.

A = Pink (P)   P = White (W)   I = Grey (G)

If the amount is missing, add W + G.
If the interest is missing, subtract W from P.
If the principal is missing, subtract G from P.

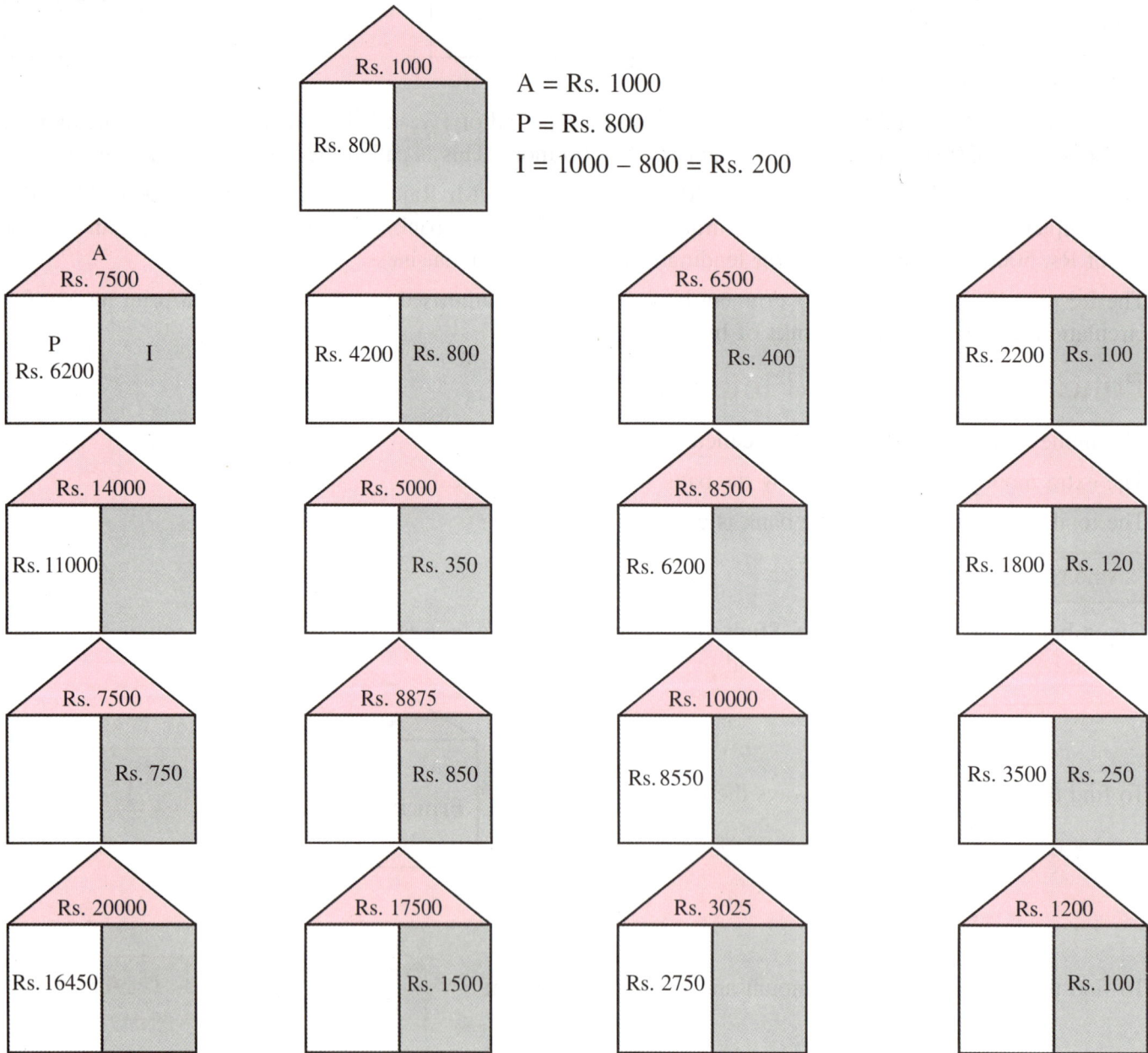

Interest is normally paid as a percentage. You have already learnt about percentage. 'Per' means 'out of' and 'cent' means 100. So 'percentage' means 'out of 100'. The symbol used for percentage is '%'.

When the bank makes a commitment to pay you interest, it is always paid as a percentage, usually for a period of one year. This % of interest is called the 'rate'. Suppose, you deposit Rs. 40,000 in the bank at the rate of 10% interest. How much will you get back after one year?

Amount = 40,000 + 10% of 40,000 ('of' is used to denote multiplication.)
So, first find out what is 10% of 40,000.

$$\frac{10}{100} \times \frac{40000}{1} = \frac{10 \times 400}{1} = Rs.\ 4000.$$

> **Remember!**
> 1 is the denominator for whole numbers.

This is called simple interest.
(You can cancel the zeroes in the numerator and denominator and simplify the fraction.)
So,   A = P + I = 40,000 + 4000 = Rs. 44,000

If the time or period is not mentioned, then it should be taken as 1 year.
To solve a problem on simple interest, you should know the following formula.

$$I = \frac{Principal \times Period \times Rate}{100}$$

Example

Find the simple interest on Rs. 4000 for 2 years at 8% interest per annum. What will be the amount paid at the end of 2 years?

    Principal = Rs. 4000   Rate = 8%   Period = 2 years

$$S.I. = 4000 \times 2 \times \frac{8}{100} = Rs.\ 640$$

Amount = P + I = 4000 + 640 = Rs. 4,640

Exercise 2

Complete the following.

Principal	Rate of interest	Time/Period	Interest	Amount
Rs. 5500	4%	1 year		
Rs. 8000	6%	2 years		
Rs. 6500	5%	2 years		
Rs. 10,000	10%	3 years		
Rs. 7500	3%	4 years		
Rs. 5000	12%	1 year		
Rs. 15,000	11%	2 years		
Rs. 9500	9%	5 years		
Rs. 20,000	8%	2 years		

If the rate is a mixed number, what do you do?

Look at this.

Lata borrowed Rs. 4000 for a period of 2 years at $2\frac{1}{2}$% rate of interest. Find the interest and the amount.

So, $I = \dfrac{P \times T \times R}{100} = \dfrac{4000 \times 2 \times 2\frac{1}{2}}{100} = \dfrac{4000 \times 2 \times \frac{5}{2}}{100}$

You get $I = \dfrac{40\cancel{00} \times \cancel{2} \times 5}{\cancel{100} \times \cancel{2}} = 40 \times 5 = $ Rs. 200

Interest = Rs. 200

Amount = Rs. 4000 + Rs. 200 = Rs. 4200

Exercise 3

Now complete the following table.

Principal	Rate of interest	Time/period	Interest	Amount
Rs. 2000	$2\frac{1}{2}$ %	1 year		
Rs. 4500	$3\frac{1}{4}$ %	2 years		
Rs. 5000	$4\frac{1}{2}$ %	1 year		
Rs. 8000	$1\frac{3}{4}$ %	3 years		
Rs. 10,000	$5\frac{1}{2}$ %	4 years		

Fractions, Decimals and Percentage

There is a relationship between fractions, decimals and percentage. To understand it, let us consider the following comparison.

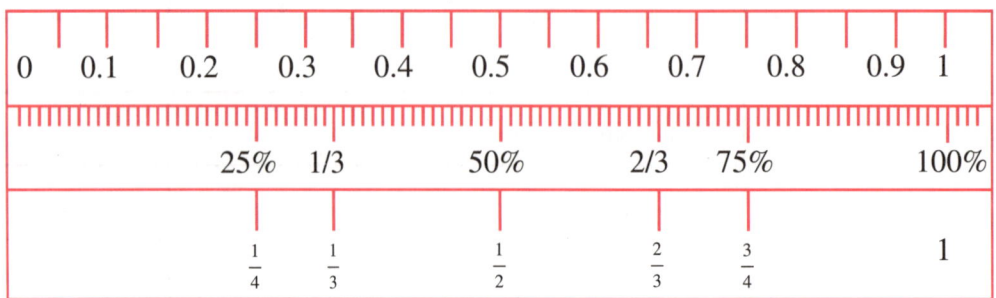

- The first strip shows one whole divided into 10 parts. So each is $\dfrac{1}{10}$ or 0.1 in decimals.
- The second strip is divided into 100 parts to show percentage.

- The third strip is divided into four parts to show 1 whole and its fractions $\frac{1}{4}, \frac{1}{3}, \frac{1}{2}, \frac{2}{3}, \frac{3}{4}$.

| $\frac{1}{4} = 25\% = 0.25$ | $\frac{1}{2} = 50\% = 0.5$ | $\frac{3}{4} = 75\% = 0.75$ | 1 whole = 100% = 1.0 |

You can use the middle line, which has been divided into 100 parts, to find the equivalent fraction and decimal for a given percentage. Use a foot ruler, aligning it from top to bottom, and find out.

Converting Fractions to Percentage

To change the fractions to per cent, multiply by 100.

Exercise 4

Now change the following fractions to percentage. One has been done for you.

(a) $\frac{1}{2} = \frac{1}{2} \times 100 = 50\%$ (b) $\frac{3}{5} =$ (c) $\frac{1}{4} =$

(d) $\frac{4}{5} =$ (e) $\frac{7}{10} =$ (f) $\frac{1}{8} =$

Converting Decimals to Percentage

To change the decimals to per cent, convert the decimal to fraction and multiply by 100.

Exercise 5

Now change the following decimals to percentage. One has been done for you.

(a) $0.5 = \frac{5}{10} \times 100 = \frac{500}{10} = 50\%$ (b) $0.6 =$ (c) $0.3 =$

(d) $0.12 =$ (e) $0.25 =$ (f) $0.8 =$

Word Attack

(a) Raghu borrowed Rs. 15,000 from his friend for a period of 3 years at an interest rate of 3%. How much interest will he have to pay? What amount will he have to return at the end of 3 years?

(b) Shanaz gave Rs. 25,000 to her friend for 2 years at the rate of 7% interest per annum. Her friend returned only Rs. 22,000. How much more is she supposed to return?

(c) Jayesh got a loan of Rs. 13,500 from his friend to repair his house. He promised to return Rs. 15,000 at the end of the year. How much extra money did he return and what % of the principal does it represent?

(d) Aditya deposited Rs. 4000 in the bank for a period of 3 years. The bank gave him an interest at the rate of $2\frac{1}{2}$% per year. He collected the amount after 3 years and again deposited it for a year at $2\frac{1}{2}$% interest. How much money did he get at the end of the year?

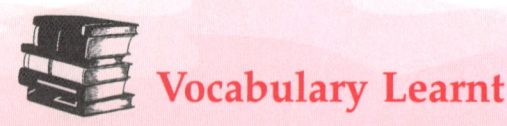

Vocabulary Learnt

percentage   interest   principal

amount   rate

deposit   lend   incentive

Chapter 13 Unitary Method

> **You know...**
> - how to buy things from a shop
> - the cost of two or more things will be more than the cost of one.

Understanding Unitary Method

The word 'unit' means one. The term **unitary method** has evolved from this concept. This topic is all about finding the cost of two or more things when the cost of one is given and vice versa.

Example 1

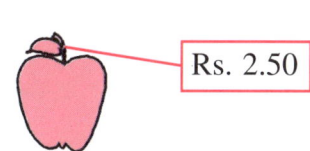
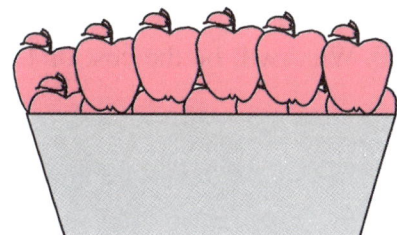

Here you see that the cost of one apple is marked as Rs. 2.50. There is a basket of 13 apples next to it. What do you think will be their cost?

Will the cost of the apples in the basket be more or less as compared to that of one apple?

What operation will you use to find it out?

The cost of apples in the basket will be more. You multiply the cost of one apple by the number of apples to find the total cost of apples.

So, the cost of 13 apples = 13 × 2.50 = Rs. 32.50.

Example 2

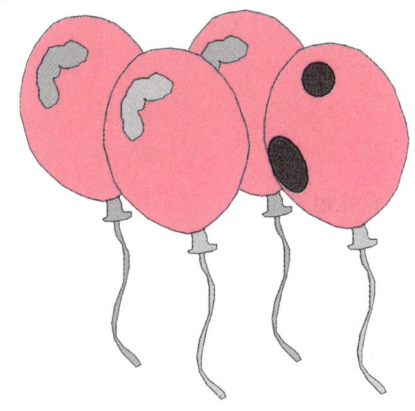
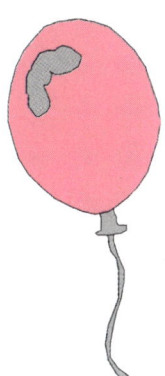

If Tom paid Rs. 14.00 for 4 balloons, how much would he pay for one balloon?

Will the cost of one balloon be more or less as compared to that of four?

What operation will you use to find it out?

The cost of one balloon will be less. You divide the total cost of balloons by the number of balloons, i.e., 4, to find the cost of one balloon.

So, the cost of one balloon = 14 ÷ 4 = Rs. 3.50.

Exercises in unitary method are given in the form of word attack. So, it is very important to read the problems carefully to decide whether to use multiplication or division to solve the problem.

Hence, remember the following procedure.

(a) Find the facts.

(b) Find the question.

(c) Find the operation to use.

(d) Give reasons for choosing the operation.

Exercise 1

Write the statements and solve.

(a) The cost of 6 balls is Rs. 90.00. What will be the cost of 1 ball?

(b) A bucket can hold 29 litres of water. How much water can 18 such buckets hold?

(c) The cost of 120 mangoes is Rs. 420.00. What will be the cost of 1 mango?

(d) If a cow gives 143 litres of milk in 13 days, how much milk will it give in 1 day?

(e) 4 baskets of fruits cost Rs. 2484.00. What is the cost of 1 basket?

(f) A man works for 17 days and earns Rs. 306.00. What is his daily wage?

Direct Variation

Direct Variation is when two things or two quantities are related to each other in such a way that an increase in one will result in an increase in the other, or a decrease in one will result in a decrease in the other. In other words, a direct change in one will result in a similar change in the other.

Example 1

The cost of 1 book = Rs. 5.00.

The cost of 5 such books will be = Rs. 25.00.

The cost of 10 such books will be = Rs. 50.00.

The cost of 2 such books will be = Rs. 10.00.

Do you notice that the cost goes up when the number of books increase and the cost comes down when the number of books decrease?

This is direct variation.

Example 2

The cost of 12 books is Rs. 24.00. What will be the cost of 15 books?

You already know that in direct variation, if one goes up, the other also goes up. Since the number of books has gone up from 12 to 15, the cost should also increase from Rs. 24.00.

How do you find out the answer?

There are two ways of finding the answer.

Method 1

Cost of 12 books = Rs. 24.00.

Cost of 1 book = 24 ÷ 12 = Rs. 2.00.

Cost of 15 books = 15 × 2 = Rs. 30.00.

Method 2

You have already studied about ratio, where you learnt about direct proportion and inverse proportion. So you should use that knowledge here. Let us assume the cost of 15 books to be x. There are two variables in this problem.

(a) The number of books.

(b) The total cost.

So we write,

No. of books	Total cost	No. of books	Total cost
12	24	15	x

They are said to be in proportion. So, we write 12 : 24 :: 15 : x

When the two ratios are proportionate, the product of the two extremes, that is $12 \times x$, will be equal to the product of the two means, that is, 24 and 15.

So this is how you should find the value of 'x'.

$$12 \times x = 24 \times 15$$

$$\text{So, } 12x = 360$$

If $12x = 360$,

then $x = 360 \div 12 = 30$

So the value of x is 30.

To check, find the product of 12×30 and 24×15 and see if they are the same.

Are they the same? _____.

The variable may be at any place in the ratio. So you should read carefully and write in such a way that it corresponds with what it is related to.

Example 3

A bus travels 125 km in 5 hours. What distance can it travel in 8 hours at the same speed?

Distance	Time taken	Distance	Time taken
125 km	5 hrs	x	8 hrs

So you write, $125 : 5 :: x : 8$

$$125 \times 8 = 5 \times x$$

$$\text{So, } 5 \times x = 125 \times 8$$

$$5x = 1000 \Rightarrow x = 1000 \div 5$$

So, $x = 200$

Check

$125 \times 8 = 1000$ and $200 \times 5 = 1000$.

Your answer is correct.

Here are some rules to remember while working with direct variation.

(a) The two sets of ratios must be proportionate.

(b) 'x' should correspond to the unknown variable.

(c) If the term corresponding to 'x' increases or decreases, the value of 'x' should accordingly increase or decrease in the answer.

Exercise 2

Look at these examples.

(a) $12 : 24 :: 6 : x$ Here, 24 is bigger than 12. So 'x' should be bigger than 6.

(b) $9 : 6 :: x : 12$ Here, 9 is bigger than 6. So, 'x' should also be bigger than 12.

(c) $x : 24 :: 18 : 36$ Here, 18 is smaller than 36. So, 'x' should also be smaller than 24.

(d) $9 : x :: 10 : 20$ Here, 20 is bigger than 10. So, 'x' should also be bigger than 9.

Now solve the following problems.

(a) 36 apples cost Rs. 216.00. What will be the cost of 14 such apples?

(b) Govind worked for 5 days and earned Rs. 1245.00. How much will he earn if he works for 11 days?

(c) The cost of a dozen eggs is Rs. 24.00. What will be the cost of 19 eggs?

(d) Ramu bought 13 kg of rice for Rs. 292.50. How much rice can be bought for Rs. 382.50?

(e) In 4 hours, Sailesh can read 240 pages. In how many hours can he read 540 such pages?

(f) David worked for 2 months and saved Rs. 540.00. How much will he save if he works for 5 months?

Inverse Proportion

Inverse proportion is slightly different from direct variation.

Look at this example to understand inverse proportion.

Example 1

If 8 men take 10 days to finish a job, how long would it take for 10 men to finish the same job?

Here, it is important to assume that all men have the same capacity. So, when more men are put on the job, naturally the work will get done faster. So more men means less time is taken to finish the job.

When one variable increases, the other will decrease and, when one variable decreases, the other will increase.

Look at another example of inverse proportion.

Example 2

A bus covers a certain distance in 3 hours at a speed of 40 km/hr. How long will it take to cover the same distance at the speed of 60 km/hr?

(a) Is the bus travelling faster, slower or at the same speed in the question? _____

(b) Will the bus take more time or less time at the speed of 60 km/hr? Give reasons for your answer.

_____

_____

When the bus increases its speed, it is bound to take less time. This is **inverse proportion**, because one increases and the other decreases.

How do you find out?

Look at this.

$$3 : 40 \ :: \ x : 60$$

In inverse proportion, the product of the first two terms should be equal to the product of the next two terms.

i.e., $\quad 3 \times 40 = x \times 60$

$\Rightarrow \quad\quad 120 = 60x$ or $60x = 120$

So, $\quad\quad x = 120 \div 60 = 2$ hours

Check

3×40 should be equal to 2×60.

Are they the same? _____.

Here are some rules to remember while working with inverse proportion.

(a) When one variable increases, the other should decrease.

(b) 'x' should always correspond to the missing term.

(c) If the term corresponding to 'x' increases, x should decrease. If the term corresponding to 'x' decreases, x should increase.

Exercise 3

Now solve the following.

(a) 8 men can do a piece of work in 6 days. How many men can do the same work in 4 days?

(b) A train travels for 2 hours and covers a distance at a speed of 50 km/hr. If it travels at a speed of 80 km/hr, how much time will it take to cover the same distance?

(c) 6 men can do a piece of work in 5 days. How many days are needed to finish the same work, if 4 men do it?

(d) 8 persons plough a field in 12 hours. How many hours will it take for 12 persons to plough the same field?

Maths Lab Activity 1

Material required

(a) Story cards like the ones given below
(b) Picture cards as shown on the next page

Method (Note for the Teacher)

Distribute the story cards to the students. Ask them to read them carefully and tell whether they would use division or multiplication to solve the problems. Giving the answers is not so important now; it is more essential to know what operation to use.

| One chocolate costs Rs. ◯ So, 7 chocolates cost Rs. 64.75. | Priya took ◯ pictures in 1 day. She can take 250 pictures in 2 days. |

John bakes 16 doughnuts in one day. He can bake ◯ doughnuts in 5 days.

Priya baked ◯ cookies in a day. In 5 days, she can bake 130 cookies.

8 books cost Rs. 24.00. So ◯ books will cost Rs. 36.00.

Distribute the picture cards and ask the students to create their own stories using direct variation.
The same cards may be used another day to work out the answers.

Chapter 14

Bills

> **You know...**
> - things are bought by paying cash
> - we buy only the amount we need
> - we pay only as much as the product costs
> - we check the bill to find out the price we need to pay for a product.

All items are measured by their quantity (length, volume, weight) and by their value. Generally, things are manufactured and sold to meet the needs of the customer. For example, you can get a 50 gm toothpaste tube for your travel kit as well as a 200 gm family pack of toothpaste for daily use at home. When we shop, we buy according to the need and with a budget in mind. The traders who make these available to us are registered with the government. They need to have regular bills and accounting systems in place to show what they sell and how much they earn.

Bills are very important, both for the trader and the customer. They help the traders in listing the items sold and the money collected by them. They also help the customer check the prices and the amount charged.

Generally, bills have the following details.

(a) Name and address of the shop.
(b) The bill number to help the customer trace back any details later.
(c) Names of items with their quantities.
(d) The rate at which the items are sold.
(e) The sum of the prices of the items.
(f) Other charges or taxes which may be charged (sometimes).

Now let us look at a few samples of bills.

(a) Grocery store   (b) Vegetable and fruit market   (c) General store

A.G. Grocers
45, MG Road, Pune

Bill: 567   Date: 10/10/2006

Item	Quantity	Rate per kg	Value
Gold Winner oil	1 kg	56.00	56.00
Coffee powder	500 gm	130.00	65.00
Sugar	2 kg	19.50	39.00
Gram dal	1 kg	48.00	48.00
		Total	208.00

Fruit Drip Stores
Sardar Patel Road, Bangalore – 560083

Bill: 1089   Date: 01/06/2005

Item	Quantity	Rate	Amount
Cauliflower	1	20 (each)	20.00
Mangoes	6	48/dozen	24.00
Potato	1.5 kg	12/kg	18.00
Tomato	500 gm	16/kg	8.00
Banana	3	Rs. 3/banana	9.00
Beans	300 gm	18/kg	5.40
		Total	84.40

TNGST No. 12782/OE   CST No.3352/02

Food World Super Market
East Coast Road Tiruvanmiyur, Chennai – 41

PH: 24483795

Bill: 7253/3   Date: 11/03/2005

Item	Quantity	Rate per unit	Amount
Brylcream	100 gm	45.00	45.00
Apple juice	1 litre bottle	93.00	93.00
Wheat	2.5 kg	18.00	45.00
Mustard	100 gm	6.00	6.00
Cooking butter	500 gm	65.00	65.00
Ice cream	1 litre	110.00	110.00
Strawberry juice	1.7 litre	40.00	68.00
Ketchup	200 ml	28.00	28.00
		Total	460.00

Word Attack

Make bills for the following and find the total cost in each case.

(a) Shiva went to Rajaram Provision Store and bought 2 kg of tuar dal at Rs. 23.50 per kg, 3 ½ kg of moong dal at Rs. 41.70 per kg, 5 kg of rice at Rs. 22.00 per kg, 100 g of mustard at Rs. 15 per kg and 250 g of jeera at Rs. 20 per kg. Prepare a bill and find the total cost. Find out how much he should get back, if he gives a 500 rupee note to the shopkeeper.

(b) Sanjay went to a cloth shop to buy dress materials for his family for Diwali. He bought 4 m of cloth for trousers at Rs. 215 per metre, 5.2 m of shirt material at Rs. 90 per metre, a silk saree for his wife for Rs. 2150 and 2 synthetic sarees, at the rate of Rs. 495 per saree, for his two sisters. How much was the total bill amount?

(c) Sonali went to the fruit market to buy fruits to make fruit salad for her daughter's birthday. She bought 6 apples at the rate of Rs. 12 per apple, 4 oranges at Rs. 3 per piece, ½ kg of grapes at Rs. 32 per kg and 6 bananas at Rs. 18 per dozen. What is her total expenditure?

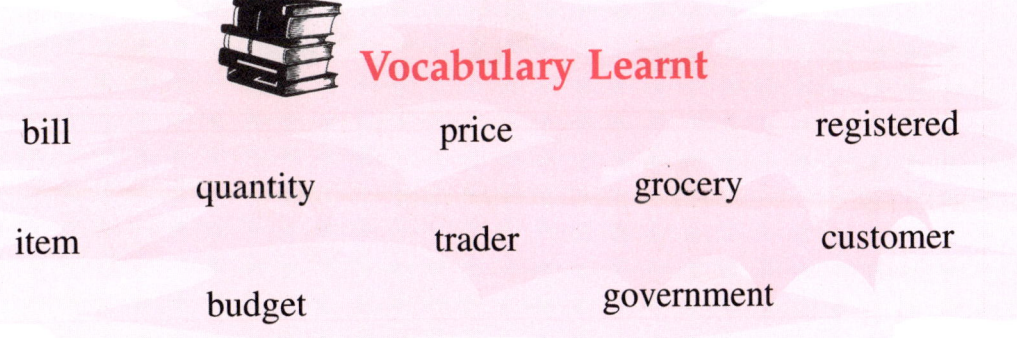

Vocabulary Learnt

bill   price   registered

quantity   grocery

item   trader   customer

budget   government

Maths Lab Activity 1

Materials required

(a) A big display card with pictures of dresses and their individual prices, as shown below.

(b) Several strips of cards with only pictures of a few of the dresses on each of them, as shown below.

Method (Note for the Teacher)

Put the big chart up on display. Give every two students a strip of card. Ask them to look at their cards very carefully and find out which of the clothes from the display card are there in their card. Ask them to make a bill for the clothes and find out how much they have to pay the shopkeeper. Go around and check if they are following all the steps required to make a bill.

Display Chart

Shirt	Apron	Short jacket	Skirt top	Shorts
Rs. 345	Rs. 216	Rs. 199	Rs. 89	Rs. 586
Muffler	Jeans	Skirt	Trouser	Scarf	Shirt
Rs. 129	Rs. 765	Rs. 888	Rs. 320	Rs. 257	Rs. 965

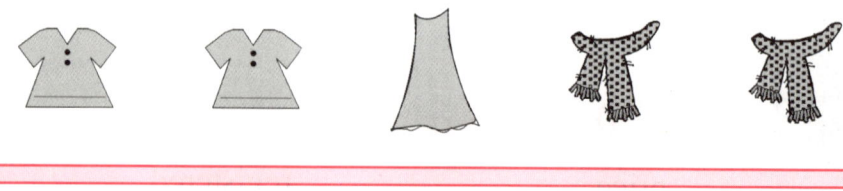

Chapter 15

Time

> **You know...**
> - time can be measured by using different apparatus
> - time is relative
> - time can be grouped into different periods like year, century and millennium.

You have already learnt about 'time' in the previous classes and, by now, all of you know how important it is to recognise its significance.

Time can be measured by using several devices. We also know time is relative. When we are involved in activities that interest us, time seems to move fast. But, when we are doing something not so interesting, time seems to move very slowly.

You can take a quick look at what you already know about time.

Time on a Clock

Exercise 1

Mark the given time on the clocks by drawing the hour hand and the minute hand on each.

(a) 8 : 52

(b) 11 : 48

(c) 7 : 13

(d) 6 : 22

(e) 3 : 59

(f) 9 : 16

Exercise 2

What time is shown by each clock given below? Write the approximate answer in the box given below each.

(a)

(b)

(c)

(d)

(e)
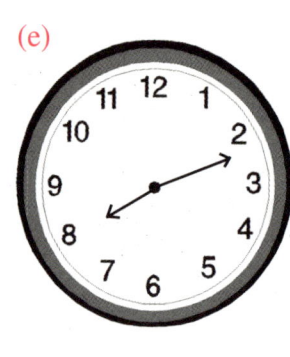

(f)

Time and Seasons

Why do seasons occur?

The seasons occur because of the movement of the Earth around the Sun. There are four seasons – spring, summer, autumn and winter.

In spring, the snow melts and the farmers get ready to plant seeds.

In summer, the plants begin to grow bigger and it is time to reap.

In autumn, the leaves change colour and begin to wither, and animals get busy storing food.

In winter, it is very cold and it begins to snow, and animals start searching for warm places to sleep.

Maths Lab Activity 1

Materials required

(a) A rectangular piece of chart paper (40 cm × 10 cm) (b) Pencil (c) Crayons

Method

Divide the chart into four equal parts and mark the parts as spring, summer, autumn and winter respectively. Under each heading, draw a picture to show the season, preferably a tree with things around. Now turn the paper to the other side, and write down all the sentences that go with the season you have drawn. To help you, some sentences are given below. You can choose some from there and add your own.

Spring	Summer	Autumn	Winter
			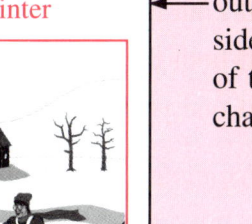

← outer side of the chart

(a) The trees become bare.
(b) Animals search for warm places to sleep.
(c) The trees are in full bloom.
(d) The days are short and the nights are long.
(e) The snow starts melting.
(f) The farmers sow seeds in the fields.
(g) The leaves wither and fall.
(h) Animals begin to store food.
(i) The plants begin to grow bigger.
(j) Some leaves change colour.
(k) The air gets warm and the days are long.
(l) The sun becomes scorching hot.
(m) Birds start migrating

Time and Calendar

You have already learnt about days, weeks, months and year.

Leap Year

Every year has 365 days, but, once in every four years, we get an extra day. Such a year with 366 days is called a *leap year*.

Why do we have a leap year?

This is because there are nearly 365 ¼ days in a year (365 and 969/4000 days). For the sake of convenience, the odd portion, which is nearly ¼ day, is taken forward every year for 4 consecutive years and added together as one day to the fourth year. So there are 366 days every fourth year.

Find out to which month this extra day is added. _____

The Christian Era: BC and AD

Now you will learn about BC and AD.

BC means **Before Christ**, that is, before the birth of Lord Jesus Christ.

AD means **Anno Domini** (in the year of our Lord). It starts from the year Lord Jesus Christ was born.

So, if you say 'in the year 1920 AD', it means 1920 years after the birth of Jesus.

When you say '69 BC', it means 69 years before the birth of Jesus.

How do you calculate the number of years between the two given dates?

Here are the rules.

(a) If both the given years are AD, then subtract the earlier year from the later.
(b) If both the given years are BC, subtract the later from the earlier.
(c) If one year is AD and the other is BC, add the two numbers.

Example
1. Calculate the number of years from: 42 AD to 83 AD
   83 − 42 = 41 years

2. Calculate the number of years from: 129 BC to 58 BC
   129 − 58 = 71 years

3. Calculate the number of years from: 49 BC to 29 AD
   49 + 29 = 78 years

Exercise 3

Calculate the number of years.

(a) 239 AD to 351 AD = ( )
(b) 1256 AD to 1498 AD = ( )
(c) 249 BC to 159 BC = ( )
(d) 123 BC to 247 AD = ( )
(e) 111 BC to 193 BC = ( )
(f) 23 BC to 123 AD = ( )

February has 29 days in a leap year. To find out whether it is a leap year or not, use the test of divisibility by 4.

If the last two digits are zero or the number is divisible by 4, then it is a leap year.

Now, in which year were you born? _____

Was it a leap year? _____

Century

A century has 100 years. The first century is the period of time from year 1 to year 100. The second century is from year 101 to 200 and so on. In which century are we living? _____

Have you heard the word century used anywhere else? Give two examples.

(a) _____   (b) _____

Millennium

A period of thousand years is called a millennium. We are going through the third millennium, which began on the 1st of January, 2001. In order to correct the marginal difference between ¼ of a day (approximation while calculating the leap year) and 969/4000 parts of a day (which is the actual extra part of the year over 365 days), once in every 4000 years, a leap year will be dropped.

24 Hour Clock

Usually, we use a 12 hour clock in our homes, but we all know that there are 24 hours in a day. There are clocks that show 24 divisions. Clocks with such divisions are used in railway and air timings.

In a 12 hour clock, when the hour hand goes back to 1 after 12 noon, it is taken as 1 p.m., but in a digital clock this is represented by number 13. There is no a.m. or p.m. in a digital clock. The time is expressed only as hours. The 24th hour is represented as 00:00.

Exercise 4

(a) Draw a sun if it is a.m. and a moon if it is p.m., in the given boxes.

(i) It's time for breakfast. a.m. ☀   (ii) Dinner is ready. p.m. ☾

(iii) I go for jogging, before sunrise. ☐   (iv) The last show began very late. ☐

(v) It is time for the milkman to come. ☐   (vi) I enjoyed the biryani at lunch. ☐

(vii) Bed time is at 10:00. ☐   (viii) I go out to play at 4:00 daily. ☐

(b) Convert the time given to 24 hour clock time.

(i) Jayesh is going to play football at 4 p.m. _____

(ii) The aircraft from America landed at 2 a.m. _____

(iii) Pam sat down to have dinner at 9:30 p.m. _____

(iv) The movie started at 6:30 p.m. _____

(v) I went for a walk at 6 a.m. _____

(vi) My favourite television programme starts at 7 a.m. _____

(vii) A day is complete when the clock shows 12 midnight. _____

(viii) I left for school at 7:30 a.m. _____

(ix) The sun was right on top at 12:00 noon. _____

(x) We leave school every day at 2:40 p.m. _____

(b) Convert to 12 hour clock time (a.m. or p.m.).

(i) Mom calls me for dinner at 20:00 hours every night. _____

(ii) The flight landed at 14:00 hours. _____

(iii) My day begins at 06:00 hours. _____

(iv) My dad goes for a walk at 19:00 hours every day. _____

(v) Bed time is 21:30 hours for me. _____

(vi) The rooster crows at 16:00 hours every day. _____

(vii) The newspaper boy brings the paper at 08:00 hours. _____

(viii) A new day begins at 00:00 hours. _____

(ix) My sister goes for dance classes every day at 17:00 hours. _____

(x) The train left the station at 22:50 hours. _____

Exercise 5

Fill in the boxes to tell us about your favourite television shows.

Favourite show	Channel	Day	Time	A scene from it

Word Attack

(a) Mumbai-Delhi Rajdhani Express leaves Mumbai at 20:30 hours and travels the distance in 25 hours and 40 minutes. At what time will the train reach Delhi?

(b) Nizam Express, bound for Hyderabad, starts from Bengaluru at 16:00 hours and reaches Hyderabad at 09:30 hours the next morning. What is the total time taken by the train for the journey?

(c) Chennai to Mysore-Cauvery Express takes 7 hours and 20 minutes to reach Bengaluru. After a halt for 20 minutes, it travels for 2 hours and 30 minutes to reach Mysore. If the train leaves Chennai at 11:00 hours, when will it reach Mysore?

(d) Howrah Express, from Mumbai to Howrah, makes ten halts in between the two junctions. Five of the halts take 20 minutes each and the rest of them take 40 minutes each. If the train runs for 24 hours, what is the total time of journey including the halting times?

(e) Chennai Express, leaving New Delhi at 23:10 hours, travels for 26 hours and 40 minutes. If the train leaves New Delhi on November 6, 2006 and is delayed by 1 hour and 20 minutes *en route*, when will it reach Chennai?

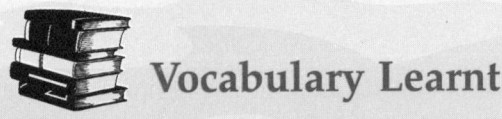
Vocabulary Learnt

leap year   Anno Domini   century

seasons   digital

millennium

Maths Lab Activity 2

Materials required

(a) A set of cards showing time on a 12 hour clock

(b) A set of cards showing corresponding time on a 24 hour clock

Method (Note for the Teacher)

Divide the students into two groups and give each group a set of cards. Ask one student from the first group to call out the time. The child from the other group who has the matching card should stand up and show his/her card. Check to see if they both show the same time. (For example, 23:10 and 11.10 p.m.) Continue the game till all have had a chance to play.

1 : 10 p.m.	13 : 10
9 : 00 p.m.	21 : 00
11 : 00 a.m.	11 : 00
12 : 10 a.m.	0 : 10

Chapter 16 Perimeter, Area and Volume

> **You know…**
> - what area and perimeter are
> - area and perimeter are measured by using different instruments like a ruler and metre scale and by calculating
> - how to estimate and find area and perimeter of geometrical figures.

Perimeter

You have already learnt all about *perimeter* in your previous class. So you can do a quick revision.

Perimeter is the total length of the boundary or the sum of all the sides of closed shapes that have straight sides.

Now look at the following shapes. How many of them have straight sides? Circle those for which the perimeter can be found easily.

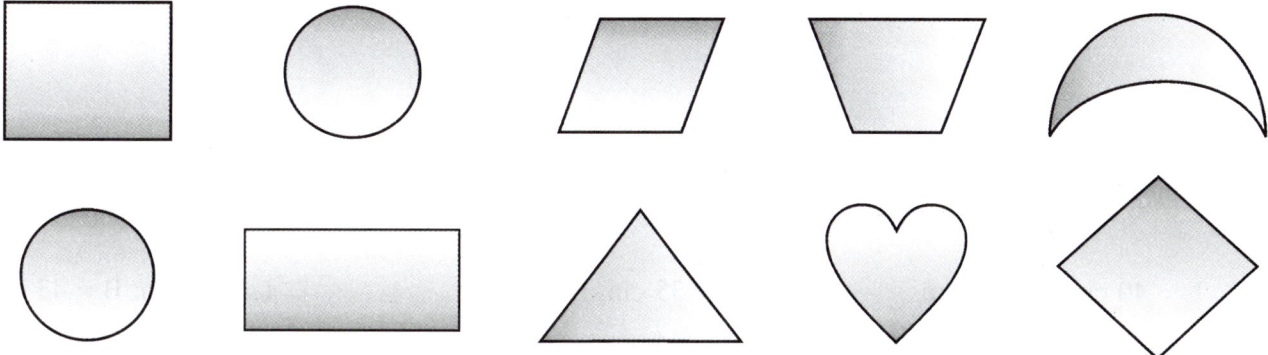

To find the perimeter, you need to know the length of each side. A ruler is used to find the measurement. In shapes like the circle and oval, there are no straight sides. So, you cannot measure them by using a ruler.

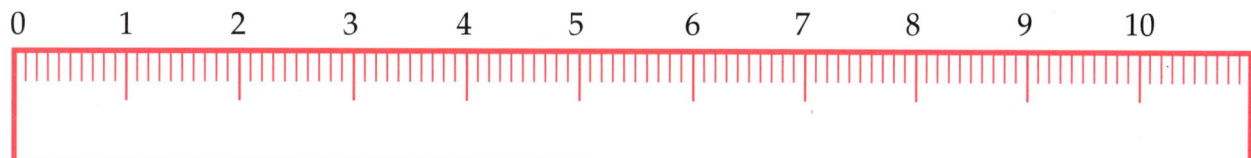

Perimeter of a Rectangle

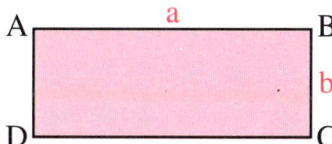

ABCD is a rectangle. It has two long sides (AB and CD) and two short sides (AD and BC). The length of its long side is 'a' and its short side is 'b'. Now, how will you find its perimeter?

There are two ways.

Method 1

If the length (L) of one side is 5 cm, the length of the other side should also be the same. In the same way, if the breadth (B) of one side is 3 cm, the breadth of the other side should also be the same. So L + L = 10 cm (5 + 5 = 10) and B + B = 6 cm (3 + 3 = 6). 2L + 2B = 16 cm (10 + 6 = 16). So the perimeter is equal to 16 cm.

Method 2

Since the opposite sides are of equal length, you can add the length and breadth of one side and multiply the sum by 2 to get the perimeter, i.e., 2 × (L + B). This is the formula for perimeter of rectangles. The sign '×' is not needed outside a bracket as it is understood that a number outside a bracket means multiplication. So, the perimeter is 2 (5 + 3), which means 2 × 8 = 16 cm.

> Perimeter of a Rectangle = 2 x (L + B)

Exercise 1

Now find the perimeter of the following rectangles by using the formula.

(a) L = 24 cm, B = 12 cm (b) L = 30 cm, B = 15 cm (c) L = 15 cm, B = 12 cm

(d) L = 40 cm, B = 25 cm (e) L = 35 cm, B = 24 cm (f) L = 60 cm, B = 43 cm

Perimeter of a Square

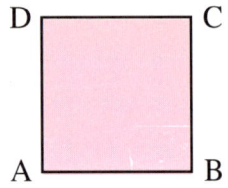

ABCD is a square. It has four equal sides. (AB, BC, CD and DA are all equal.) So, to find the perimeter, we can again use two methods.

Method 1

If the length of each side is a, then a + a + a + a = 4a (or, AB + BC + CD + DA).

Method 2

Since the length of one side of the square is a, and there are 4 such sides, you can multiply a × 4 and get '4a' as the perimeter, i.e., side × 4. This is the formula.

Exercise 2

Perimeter of a Square = 4 × side

Find the perimeter of the following squares by using the formula.

(a) side = 3 cm (b) side = 5 cm (c) side = 4.5 cm (d) side = 6.3 cm

(e) side = 7.9 cm (f) side = 11.5 cm (g) side = 14 cm (h) side = 8.8 cm

Area

Area is the measure of a closed surface. Area is generally measured in square units. Do you want to know why?

The above rectangle has been filled with circles of the same size. 27 circles have been used to cover the surface of the rectangle. But do you notice that the circles do not cover the entire surface of the rectangle? There are gaps in between.

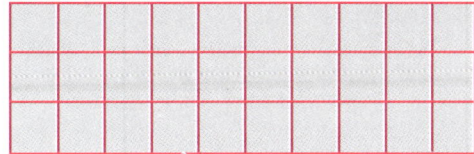

Now look at the above rectangle. The entire surface has been covered with square units. There are no gaps. It is easy to find the exact area of this rectangle, which is equal to 30 sq. units.

When shapes fit together without leaving a gap, they are tessellated.

Exercise 3

Which of the following shapes can tessellate? Colour them.

Use the above coloured shapes to make tessellating patterns of your own.

You must remember that, depending on the total surface you are measuring only units such as square cm, inches, feet and metre are used as standard units for finding the area of a shape.

So the units used for measuring the area of squares and rectangles should only be square units and the area must also be expressed only in square units.

Example

To find the area of a book, we may use a square centimetre.

To find the area of a door, we may use a square foot.

To find the area of a playground, we may use a square metre.

To find the area of a city, we may use a square kilometre.

Area of a Square

Look at this example.

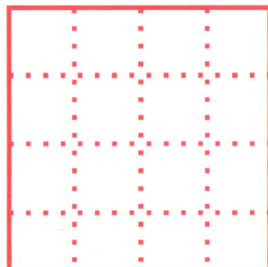

Let us use centimetre squares to find the area of this square. You can fit 16 cm squares. So we say the area of this square is 16 square cm. There are other ways of finding the area.

There are 4 squares in a row and there are 4 rows in all. Since we have 4 times 4, we multiply 4 × 4 and we get 16. In other words multiply the length by the breadth. Since both the length and breadth of a square are of same measure, A = side × side, where 'side' is the length of any one side.

Exercise 4

(a) Find the area of these figures by using unit squares. (The measurements are not accurate.)

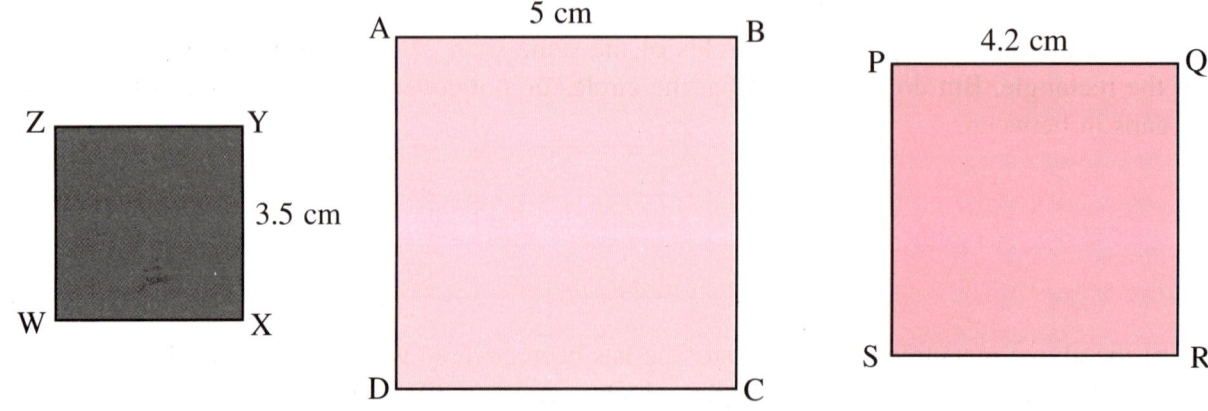

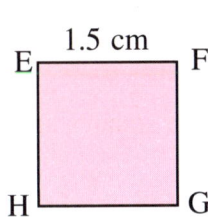 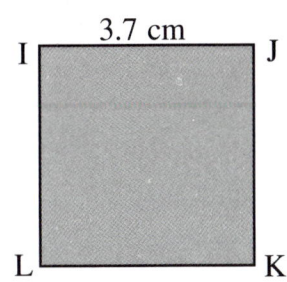 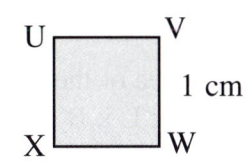

(b) Do you think we can find the area without drawing the squares? Calculate the area of the following squares by using the formula.

| Area of a Square = side x side |

(i) side = 4.5 cm   (ii) side = 6.7 cm   (iii) side = 7.9 cm   (iv) side = 8 cm

(v) side = 12 cm   (vi) side = 23 cm   (vii) side = 22.5 cm   (viii) side = 32 cm

(ix) side = 5 cm   (x) side = 20 km   (xi) side = 15.5 cm   (xii) side = 10 m

Area of a Rectangle

Since you already know how to find area, you can use the same formula to find the area of a rectangle. Look at this rectangle. It has L = 8 cm and B = 4 cm.

$A = L \times B$

So,   L × B = 8 × 4 = 32 sq. cm.

> Area of a Rectangle
> = length x breadth

Exercise 5

(a) Find the area of the rectangles of the dimensions given below by drawing 1 cm squares and then check by multiplying L × B to see if you get the same answer.

(i) 3 cm × 2 cm

(ii) 4 cm × 3 cm

(iii) 4 cm × 2 cm

(iv) 5 cm × 2 cm

(b) Find the area of the rectangles with the following measurements.

Length	Breadth	Area
8 cm	5 cm	
9 cm	3 cm	
14 cm	11 cm	

It is easy to find the area when you know the length and the breadth. But how do we find the length if the breadth and area are given, or how do we find the breadth if only the length and area are given?

Look at this.

8 cm

5 cm

Length = 8 cm

Breadth = 5 cm

Area = 8 × 5 = 40 sq. cm

Let us assume that only the area (40 sq. cm) and length (8 cm) are given. First, find out 8 multiplied by which number can give you 40.

8 × 5 = 40

So, we divide 40 by 8 and get 5. Hence, the breadth is 5 cm.

In case the breadth is given and the length is missing, you divide the area by the breadth to get the length.

Exercise 6

Now fill in this column.

Length	Breadth	Area	Is it a square or a rectangle?
5 km	5 km		
	8 cm	32 sq. cm	
12 m		96 sq. m	
	11 km	121 sq. km	
32 m	24 m		
16 cm		192 sq. cm	

It is easy to find the area of shapes that have straight sides. What about some irregular shapes?

Look at the shape given below.

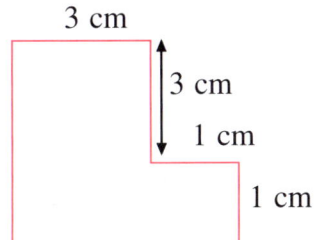

Give it a name. Now let us find its area.

Break it up into two parts: a rectangle and a square (as shown below). Find the area of each and add them up to get the total area.

Area of the rectangle = 3 × 4 = 12 sq. cm.

Area of the square = 1 × 1 = 1 sq. cm.

So, area of the full shape = 12 + 1 = 13 sq. cm.

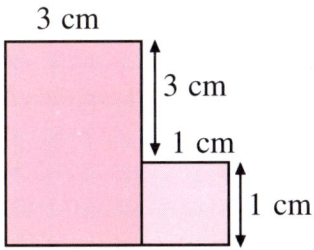

You can divide the shape in any way you want and calculate.

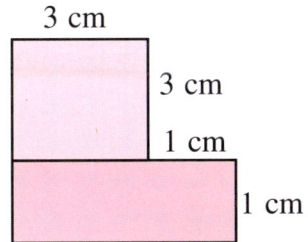

Here, Area of the square = 3 × 3 = 9 sq. cm.

Area of the rectangle = 4 × 1 = 4 sq. cm.

So, area of the full shape = 13 sq. cm.

Exercise 7

Now, find the area of the following shapes by dividing them suitably. Colour each shape in a different way.

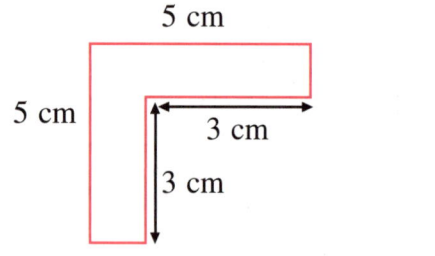 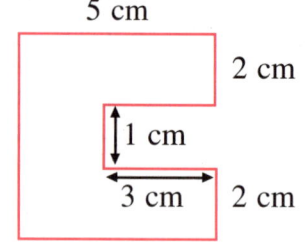 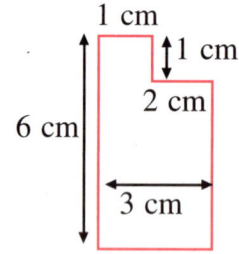

Now look at the irregular shape given below. It has no straight sides at all. How will you find its area?

You have to draw the shape on to a squared paper first, as shown.

 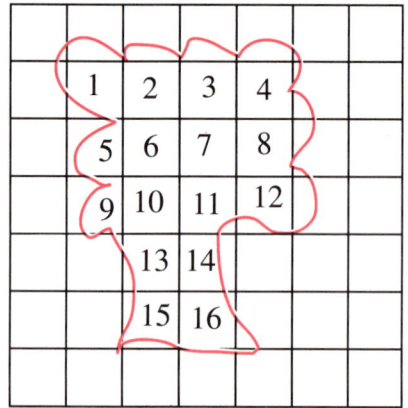

Here the picture of the tree does not cover full squares alone. Some half squares have also been used to draw the tree.

Do you know what to do?

Count every full square as one unit. Then, count all the squares that are covered half or more as one unit each. Now add them together. Area of the tree = 16 sq. units. The parts which cover less than half of a square, and therefore get left out, will partially cover for balancing the counting.

Since you do not have all full squares, area of irregular shapes can only be calculated approximately.

Exercise 8

(a) Find the area of the three irregular shapes by counting the squares.

(i) Area =   (ii) Area =   (iii) Area =

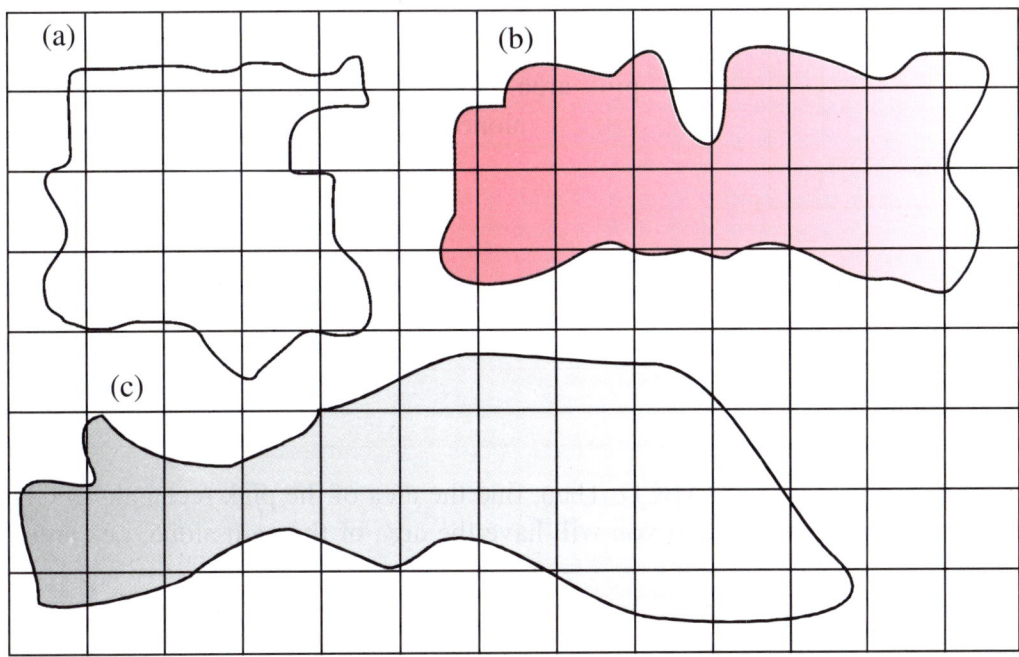

(b) Now draw irregular shapes which have the following areas.

(i) 15 sq. units   (ii) 8 sq. units   (iii) 12 sq. units   (iv) 19 sq. units

Area of Pathways

Look at this shape.

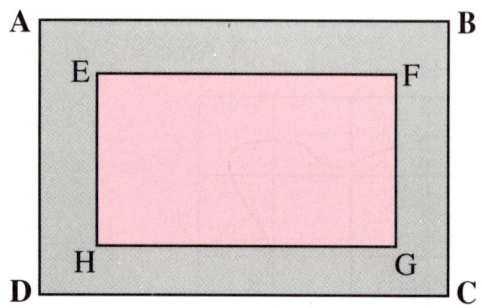

In the given picture the grey area shows a path around the pink area. Now do you think you can find the area of the pathway alone?

First, find the area of the whole rectangle ABCD. Then, find the area of the pink rectangle EFGH. Next, take away the second area from the first one and you will have the area of the path alone, i.e., area of ABCD − area of EFGH = area of the path.

Area of greater rectangle − Area of smaller rectangle = Area of the path

Exercise 9

Now, find the area of the paths in the following.

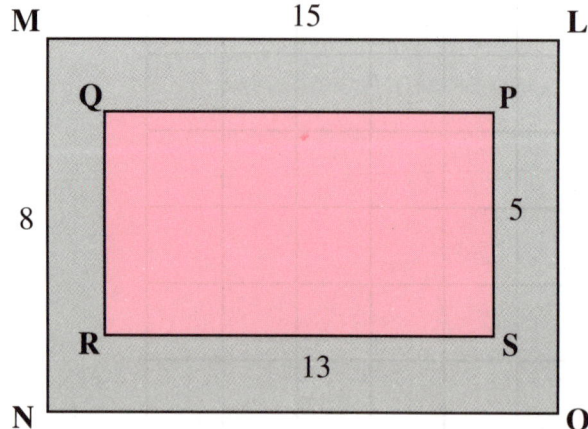

ML = NO = 15 cm
QP = RS = 13 cm
QR = PS = 5 cm
MN = LO = 8 cm

Area of the path around PQRS =

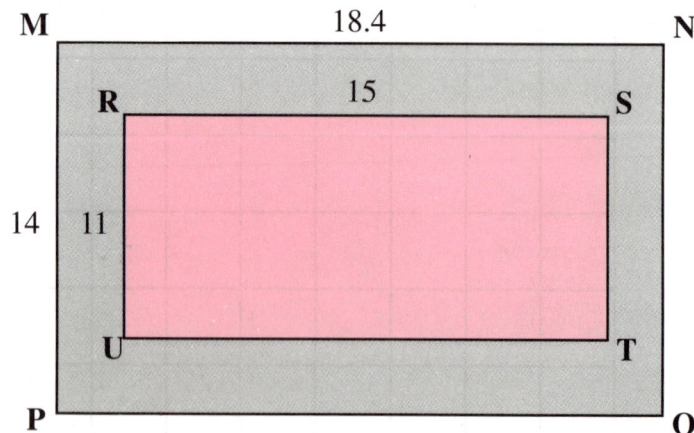

MN = PO = 18.4 cm
RS = TU = 15 cm
MP = NO = 14 cm
RU = ST = 11 cm

Area of the path around RSTU =

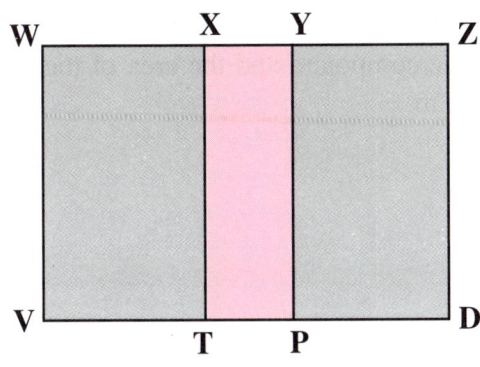
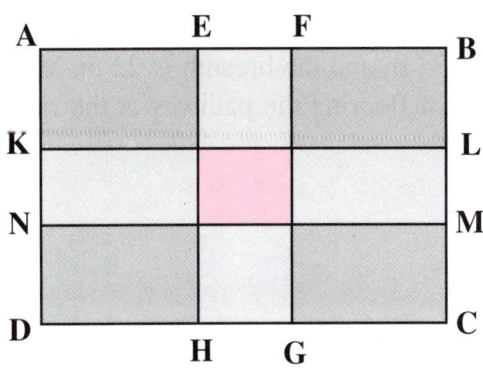

WZ = VD = 32 cm
WV = ZD = 20 cm
XY = TP = 8 cm

AB = DC = 50 cm
AD = BC = 35 cm
EF = HG = 6 cm
KN = LM = 6 cm

Area of the path XYPT = ☐

Area of the two paths together = ☐

Word Attack

Draw diagrams to help you find the answers quickly.

(a) A park is 150 m long and 120 m wide. A 4 m wide path runs along all sides inside the park. Find the area of the park and that of the path.

(b) A plot is 65 m long and 45 m wide. A path, 2.5 m wide, runs lengthwise across the middle of the plot. Find the area of the path and the area of the plot without the path.

(c) A 7 m wide pathway is laid outside the wall of a compound on all sides of a building. The length of the compound is 34 m and the breadth is 22 m. What is the area of the compound and the area of the path? Find the cost of flooring the pathway at the rate of Rs. 20 per sq. m.

(d) A field is 256 m long and 184 m wide. A pathway that is 5 m wide runs breadthwise across the field. What is the area of the field? What is the area of the path? If it costs Rs. 45.00 per sq. m to lay Korean grass on the field, leaving the pathway, how much would it cost for laying grass in the entire field?

(e) A park measuring 35 m long and 25 m wide has two paths, one running lengthwise and the other breadthwise. If the paths are 2 m wide, find the area of the park excluding the pathways.

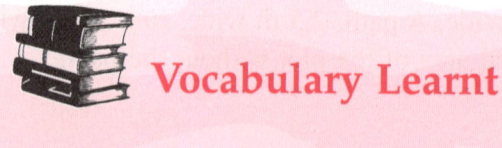

Vocabulary Learnt

area   field   compound

approximate   pathway

irregular   plot   lay

Volume

Like area, volume also is the measure of the space occupied by a shape. It is the amount of space contained in a three-dimensional shape. We generally measure the volume of liquids and gases.

However, the difference is

(a) We find the area for plane shapes and the volume of solid shapes.

(b) To find 'area' of a plane shape with straight sides, we need to know its length and breadth. But, to find the 'volume' of a shape with straight sides, we need to know its length, breadth and height.

(c) Area is a measurement of two dimensions, while volume is a measurement of three dimensions.

For which of the following shapes can you find volume? Colour only those.

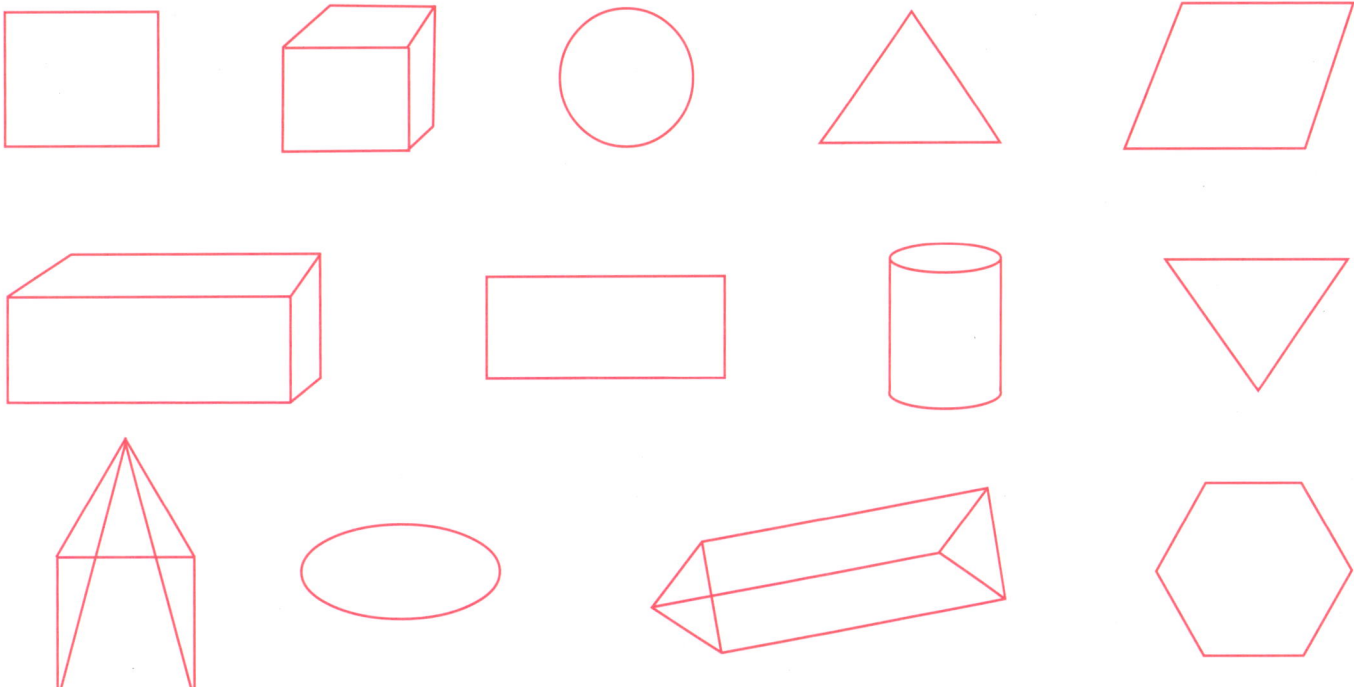

Volume of a Cube

A shape which has the same length, breadth and height is called a cube. It is made up of six square faces joined together.

We say that the side of a cube is equal to 'a' units. So, volume is equal to a × a × a = 'a' cubic units. It can also be written as a^3.

> Volume = a × a × a = a^3

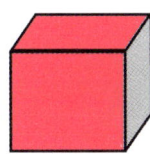

This cube is 1 cm long, 1 cm wide and 1 cm high. To find its volume, we multiply l × b × h, i.e., 1 × 1 × 1 = 1 cubic cm. This can also be written as 1^3. Since we take the three measurements, the answer should always be in cubic units.

Example

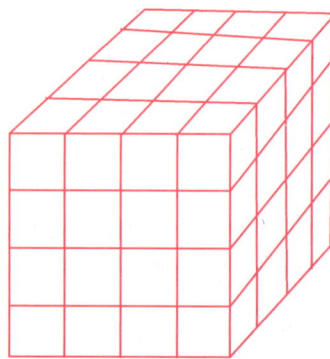

Length = 4 units.   Breadth = 4 units.   Height = 4 units.

Volume = L × B × H = 4 × 4 × 4 = 64 cubic units.

Here, each layer is built with 4 rows and each row has 4 cubes. Therefore, there are 4 × 4 = 16 cubes in a layer and there are 4 × 4 × 4 = 64 cubes in total. So, its volume = 64 cubic cm or 64 cm³.

Exercise 10

Find the volume of these cubes.

(a)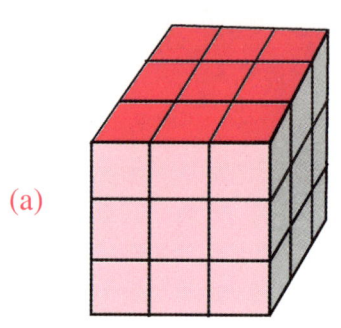

(b)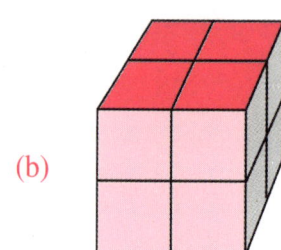

(c)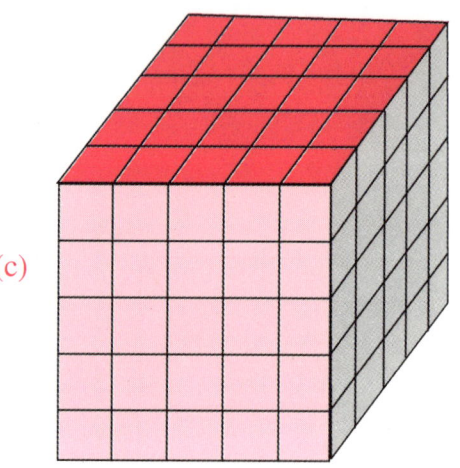

You cannot always draw to find the volume. You should be able to find the volume by using just the measurements.

For example, to find the volume of a cube with side 5.5 cm, you should use the formula,

Volume = side × side × side

Therefore,   5.5 × 5.5 × 5.5 = 166.375 cm³

> **Remember!** All measurements must be in the same unit.

> Volume = side × side × side

Exercise 11

Now find the volume for the cubes whose sides are given below.

(a) 23 cm (b) 12 cm (c) 8.5 cm (d) 10 cm (e) 11.4 cm

Volume of Cuboids

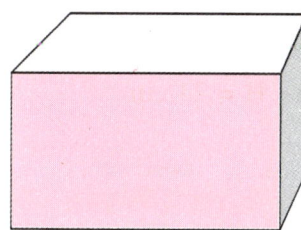 This is a cuboid. The volume of a cuboid is also found in the same way. However, unlike a cube, the sides of a cuboid are not of the same measure.

Look at this cuboid. Its length, breadth, and height are different. So, before trying to find its volume, you should measure each side carefully.

A cuboid can also be made by using cubes.

Look at this.

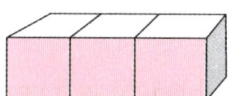 This cuboid has a length of 3 units, breadth of 1 unit and height of 1 unit.

So, its volume is L × B × H = 3 × 1 × 1 = 3 cubic units.

Exercise 12

Now answer the following.

(a) 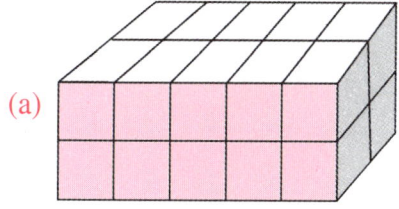 (b) 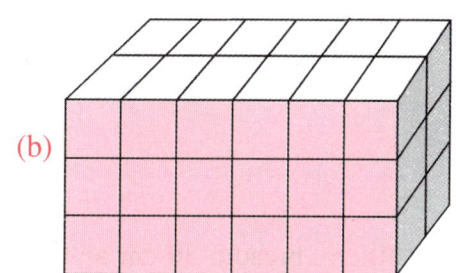 (c)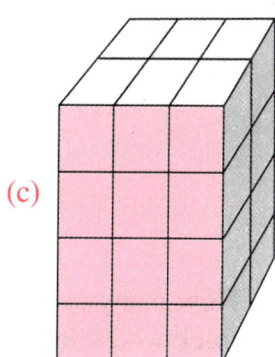

(i)   How many rows? _____   (i)   How many rows? _____   (i)   How many rows? _____

(ii) How many cubes in each row? _____   (ii) How many cubes in each row? _____   (ii) How many cubes in each row? _____

(iii) How many layers? _____   (iii) How many layers? _____   (iii) How many layers? _____

(iv) What is the volume? _____   (iv) What is the volume? _____   (iv) What is the volume? _____

Here again, you cannot always have a diagram or a model to find volume. You should use the formula and find the volume.

Volume = l × b × h

Volume can sometimes be called 'capacity' because both refer to the quantity that a container can hold.

You should also remember that while trying to do the calculations, all units of measure should be same.

For example, we cannot multiply if L = 8 m, B = 5 m and H = 112 cm. You have to change everything to cm. So, it should be changed to L = 800 cm, B = 500 cm and H = 112 cm, and then multiplied.

Exercise 13

> **Volume of Cuboid**
> $\ell \times b \times h$

Find the volume of the cuboids whose sides are given below.

(a) L = 15 cm   B = 11 cm   H = 52 cm

(b) L = 7 cm   B = 12 cm   H = 24 cm

Word Attack

(a) Find the volume of a biscuit packet whose length is 18 cm, breadth is 3 cm and height is 5 cm.

(b) Find the volume of a cargo crate whose length is 8.5 m, breadth is 5.2 m and height is 3.4 m.

(c) How many cartons with length 40 cm, breadth 30 cm and height 25 cm can be packed in a container truck whose length, breadth and height are 6m, 3m and 3m respectively?

(d) How many biscuit packets with length 10 cm, breadth 5 cm and height 4 cm can be packed in a carton whose length is 50 cm, breadth is 30 cm and height is 20 cm?

(e) How many boxes with length 70 cm, breadth 55 cm and height 39 cm can be stored in a room whose length, breadth and height are 8.4 m, 3.3 m and 3.9 m respectively?

Now you know how to find the volume when you know the length, breadth and height. But how will you find the missing measurement if you know the volume but not the measurement of one of the sides?

It is quite simple.

Look at this.

$$\text{Length} = \frac{\text{Volume}}{\text{Breadth} \times \text{Height}}$$

Similarly, $\quad \text{Breadth} = \dfrac{\text{Volume}}{\text{Length} \times \text{Height}}$

And, $\quad \text{Height} = \dfrac{\text{Volume}}{\text{Length} \times \text{Breadth}}$

Now, complete the following table.

Length	Breadth	Height	Volume
18 cm	15 cm		3220 cm³
	4 m	5 m	180 m³
20 m		20 m	8000 m³
24 mm	20 mm		57600 mm³
	16 m	11 m	1760 m³

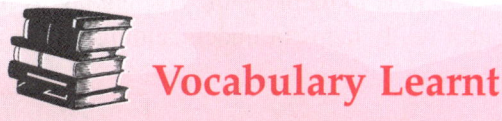

Vocabulary Learnt

capacity volume cuboid

formula cubic

dimension solid cube

Exercise 14

You have already learnt that the perimeter can be the same for two closed shapes with different areas.

(a) Ravi is drawing a games field. He measures the field to find two things, namely, perimeter and area. You already know that perimeter tells you the measurement around the field and area tells you the measurement inside the field.

(b) Here are the measurements for Ravi's field. Its area is 9 sq. m. Its perimeter is 12 m. Draw the field to a scale where 1 cm represents 1 m in your notebook.

(c) Ravi's friend, Raman wants to draw a bigger field. He wants the perimeter equal to 16 m and the area equal to 16 sq. m. What do you think you have to add to Raghu's measurements to make the field bigger? Draw a diagram to show what it will look like in your notebook.

(d) Gunjan also wants to draw a diagram with measurements of his choice. He wants the perimeter to be 14 m and the area to be 10 sq. m. What do you think should be the length and breadth of the field? Draw a sketch in your notebook.

(e) Now Priya, Raghu's sister wants her drawing to be a square which has the same number as answer for perimeter and area. What do you think should be the measurements of her square? Illustrate in your notebook.

(f) Joe is a very clever boy. He decides to draw many fields with the same area of 24 sq. m but with different perimeters. How do you think his fields will look? Draw them in your notebook.

Maths Lab Activity 1

Materials required

Nets for a few solid shapes drawn on thick cardboard for all the students

Method (Note for the Teacher)

Distribute the net for any one shape to the students and ask them to cut it out with the flaps. You should also take one and cut it out. Show to the students how to fold at each step by doing it with your net. Once the last fold has been done, help them stick the flap to complete the shape. However, before sticking the flap, ask them to look at the space created in the shape. Explain volume to them again. Try making as many shapes as possible. You may need two or three sessions for this but it really helps in understanding all the attributes of solids. Nets of some solids are given below.

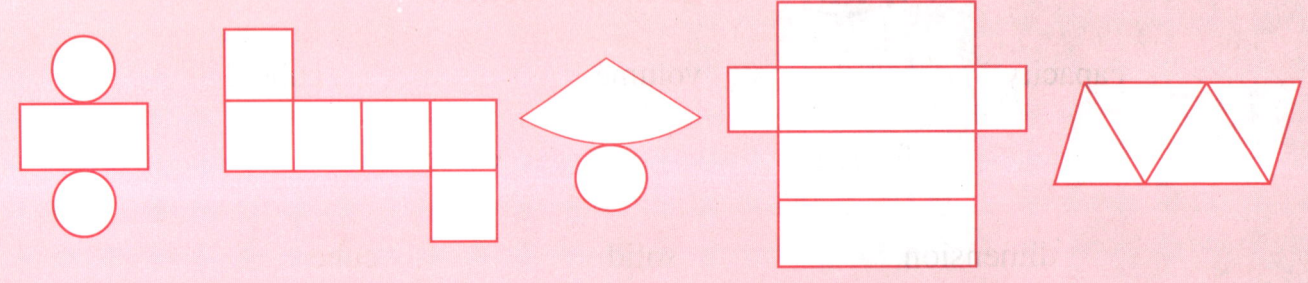

Chapter 17 — Algebra

> **You know…**
> - Arithmetic is a branch of Mathematics
> - the four basic operations involved in Arithmetic
> - there are other branches like Geometry and Algebra in Mathematics.

Algebra is a branch of Mathematics like Arithmetic and Geometry. In Arithmetic, we deal only with numbers and the four operations, while in Geometry we deal with shapes, point, line and line segments.

In Algebra, we use numbers and letters of the English alphabet to quantify numbers. These letters that take the place of numbers are called variables.

Find out the meaning of 'variable' from a dictionary and write it here.

_____

Variables do not have any fixed numerical value and, depending on the problem, their value keeps changing. Hence, they are called variables. On the other hand, numbers always have the same value and hence are called constants. This means that numbers 'always remain the same'.

Look at this example.

$$8 + x = 11$$

Here you have to find out which number, when added to 8, will give 11. It is 3.

So the value of $x = 3$ (as $8 + 3 = 11$)

Look at this example.

$$4 + x = 9$$

Here the value of $x = 5$ (as $4 + 5 = 9$)

You will notice that the value of x is 3 at one place and 5 at another place. Hence, x is called a variable. Letters can be used to express any value, in any of the operations.

Look at these algebraic expressions.

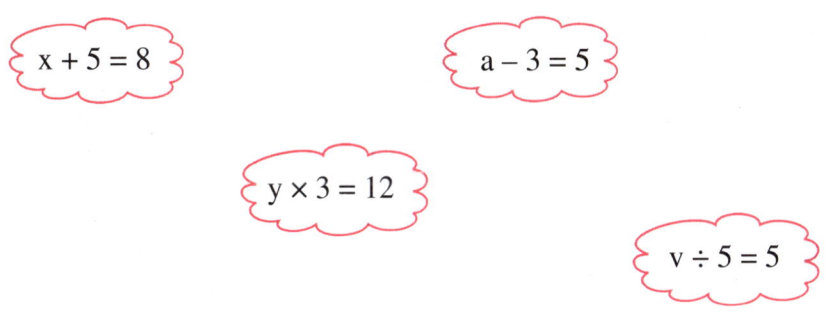

Remember!
An algebraic expression is a combination of numbers and letters formed by one or more arithmetic operations. Each expression is called a 'term'.

You know that subtraction is the opposite of addition and division is the opposite of multiplication. This fact can be employed to find the value of the variables.

$x + 5 = 8$	$a - 5 = 3$	$y \times 3 = 12$	$v \div 5 = 5$
$x = 8 - 5 = 3$	$a = 5 + 3 = 8$	$y = 12 \div 3 = 4$	$v = 5 \times 5 = 25$

You can check your answers by substituting the variable with your answer.

$x + 5 = 8$. You got 3 as your answer when you subtracted 5 from 8. So, replace x by 3.
$3 + 5 = 8$.

Now check the rest by subsituting the variables with the answers.

(a) _____

(b) _____

(c) _____

Exercise 1

Find the value of x in each.

(a) $6 + x = 9$ (b) $x + 9 = 12$ (c) $12 + x = 56$ (d) $56 + x = 142$

(e) $x - 34 = 78$ (f) $x - 45 = 89$ (g) $x - 55 = 123$ (h) $x - 78 = 67$

Every algebraic expression has one or more terms. It is the symbol that is used between them which decides how many terms are there in the expression.

Types of Expressions

Monomial – 'mono' means 'one'.
5x is a monomial expression.

Binomial – 'bi' means 'two'.
3x + y is a binomial expression.

Trinomial – 'Tri' means 'three'.
2x + 3y + z is a trinomial expression.

Polynomial – 'poly' means 'many'.
4x + 3y + 2z + 7 is a polynomial expression.

Infact, any expression with two or more than two terms is a polynomial expression.

Exercise 2

Colour according to the code given.

Monomial – yellow   Binomial – green   Polynomial – orange   Trinomial – Pink

- 3y
- 2x + 5
- 3x + 5 + 2y
- 7x + 2 + 4y + 3m
- 5 + 4z
- 7z
- 2m + 7 + 5n
- 7a + 7 + 6b + 3c
- 4s + 6t + 8
- 8z
- 2w + 8 + 5v
- 8c + 8 + 7d
- 9x + 8y + 1z + 1
- 5f + 5
- 6g + 7
- 8a
- 9 + 8x + 7y + 2z

Like and Unlike Terms

Like fractions and decimals, you can have like and unlike terms in Algebra too. Like terms are expressions that have the same variables (letters) with the same power.

Look at these.

(a) $+5a, -3a$ (b) $+2xy, -5xy$ (c) $-4y^2, +8y^2$

All these are considered like terms.

Now look at these terms.

(a) $3x^2, 4x$ (b) $+7a, -4a^2$ (c) $+8a, +4a^3$ (d) $+17b, -3x$

All these are considered unlike terms.

Like terms can be grouped together while unlike terms cannot be grouped together.

Exercise 3

Colour the like terms green and the unlike terms yellow.

- 2x + 4x
- 3z − 2y + 5x
- $7x^2 − 4x^2 + 3$
- $2b^2 + 3x^2 − y$
- $4a + 5a^2$
- 9a + 8a − a
- 9x + 4y + a
- $7a^3 − 4a^3 − 2$
- 2b + 5b − 9b
- $x^2 + 4x^2 − 8x$
- 11z + 4z − z
- 5b + 6a
- 2z + 3y − z

Exercise 4

Match the statements with their corresponding algebraic expressions by colouring the two boxes alike.

5 subtracted from x	5 × y
The product of 5 and y	(x × 3) + 7
The product of b and c	x – 5
The sum of 8 and 5, added to the sum of 9 and y	(x × 9) + (x + 2)
b multiplied by 3 and 7 added to the product	k – a
9 times m	(8 + 5) + (9 + y)
x multiplied by 3 and 7 added to the product	b × c
Tom is x years old. The age of his brother, who is 2 years younger	(5 × 3) + m
8 divided by 3 times x	x – 2
The product of 5 and 3 added to m	8 ÷ 3x
a number multiplied by 9 and the number and 2 added to that	9 × m
Minus a from k	(b × 3) + 7

Exercise 5

Change the following algebraic expressions into statements.

Example x + 5y = A number added to 5 times another number.
     b × a = The product of b and a.

(a) 2a (5 + 3) _____

(b) 6x + 3 _____

(c) m × p _____

(d) (a + b) ÷ 9 _____

(e) (k × l) ÷ 2 _____

(f) b – 6 _____

(g) n × $\frac{1}{4}$ _____

(h) (3 + 2) + y _____

(i) $2x^2$ _____

Vocabulary Learnt

Algebra   constant   variable   term   expression

monomial   binomial   trinomial   polynomial

like   unlike   branch

Maths Lab Activity 1

Materials required

(a) A few riddles based on algebraic expressions   (b) Pencil

Method (Note for the Teacher)

Develop some riddles based on algebraic expressions. One has been given below. Explain to the students how to solve them. Give one riddle to each student. Allow them to take help from each other. They can also exchange after solving their own.

Riddle

What were all the zebras going to do in the zoo? Find out by solving the following algebraic expressions and writing the letter given for each in the boxes below.

(a) $-5x + 15x - 3x =$ (b) $4x - 3x + x =$ (c) $2x + 3x - 4x =$

(d) $-x + 4x - 3x =$ (e) $2x - 3x + 5x =$ (f) $7x - 7x + x =$

(g) $9x + 2x - 4x =$ (h) $2x + 5x - x =$ (i) $4x + x - 3x =$

(j) $17x - 14x + 2x =$ (k) $2x + x - 3x =$ (l) $1x - 13x + 13x =$

1x / a

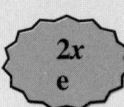
2x / e

0 / r

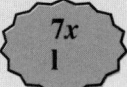
7x / l

6x / g

4x / n

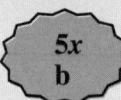
5x / b

Chapter 18 Rotation, Reflection and Nets

> **You know...**
> - that some objects like the Earth and wheel turn around on their axis
> - reflection is the reversal of an image in water or mirror
> - that net is a flat shape that can be cut and folded to make a solid shape.

Rotation

Look at the first shape given below. It can be rotated to face the four directions. Look at the second figure. It shows the shape facing the four directions in one complete rotation.

Exercise 1

Now rotate the shapes given below to face the four directions.

(a)    (b)    (c)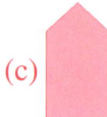

(d)    (e)    (f)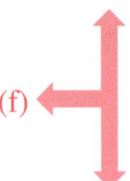

Now try this.

(a) On a sheet of paper, mark a small dot as the pivot point.

(b) Cut out a shape like the one shown in the figure.

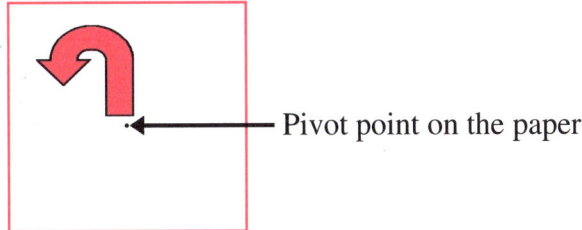
Pivot point on the paper

(c) Place one corner of the shape on the pivot point you have marked on the paper.

(d) Trace around the shape.

(e) Rotate the shape to a new position, keeping the same point of the shape on the paper's pivot point. Trace around the shape again.

(f) Continue rotating and tracing the shape until you have completed a circle.

The above design shows eight positions of the shape on rotation. You may place them very close to one another in some rotations and at a distance elsewhere to create different patterns. You may colour each shape in a different colour or just use two colours to make it look attractive. You may even rotate two different shapes around the pivotal point to make it look very attractive.

An alternate way of doing this is to cut out several pieces of the same shape and stick them on a white sheet of paper until you complete a full circle. You will then have a wonderful design.

Now cut out these shapes and try rotating them several times to see what design you get.

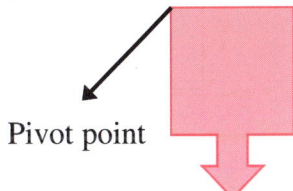
Pivot point

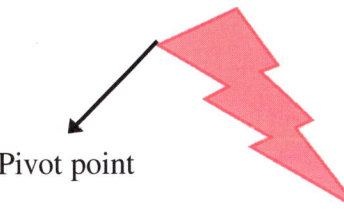
Pivot point

Reflection

A mirror image or a water image is called a reflection.

When you look at yourself in the mirror or in water, what do you notice?

Your right appears to be your left and the left appears to be right. In the reflection, things will look just the opposite of what they are. When you look in the mirror or water, the reflection you see is the reverse of yourself and what is behind you. It simply reflects the symmetry of a picture. If the mirror is not good, it can give a distorted picture that can look funny.

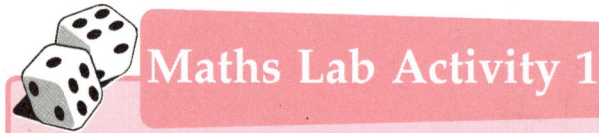

Maths Lab Activity 1

Materials required

(a) Scrapbook (b) Gum (c) Sketch pens

Method (Note for the Teacher)

Ask the students to collect pictures of reflection in water and reflection in mirror. (Some distorted mirror images can be funny.) Ask them to paste the pictures in the scrapbook and write a few lines about each.

Exercise 2

Draw the reflection of the following. They can be left to right or top to bottom, as marked.

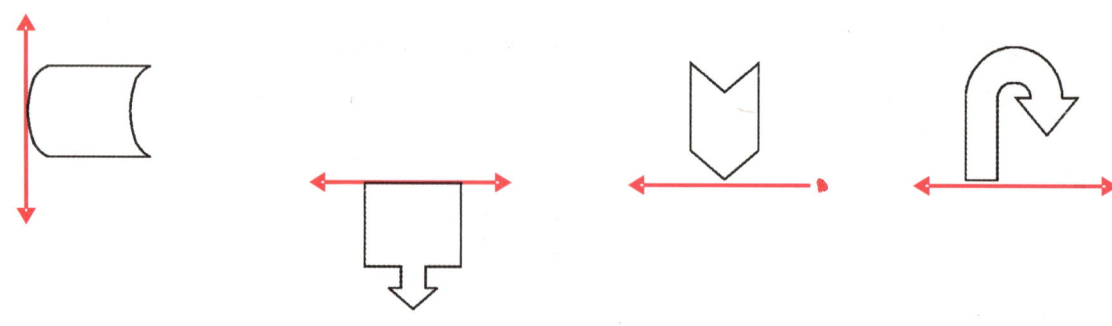

Solid Shapes and their Nets

You are going to learn about some commonly found solid shapes and their nets. In Mathematics, a **net** tells you how to draw the required shape on a flat paper and then fold on specific lines to get the solid shape. All solid shapes are called **polyhedra**.

Cube

A **cube** is the easiest solid shape to think about. All its faces are squares.

To make a net of a cube, first look at something shaped like a cube, for example, a dice.

- How many faces does it have?   Six
- What shape are they?   Squares

So, make sure that your net has six square faces. Now you must find a way to arrange the six squares so that they will fold up into a cube. There are many different ways to do this. Look at the ones given below. Some of these can be used to make a cube.

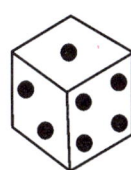

Exercise 3

(a) Which of these will form a cube? (Use ✔ or ✘)

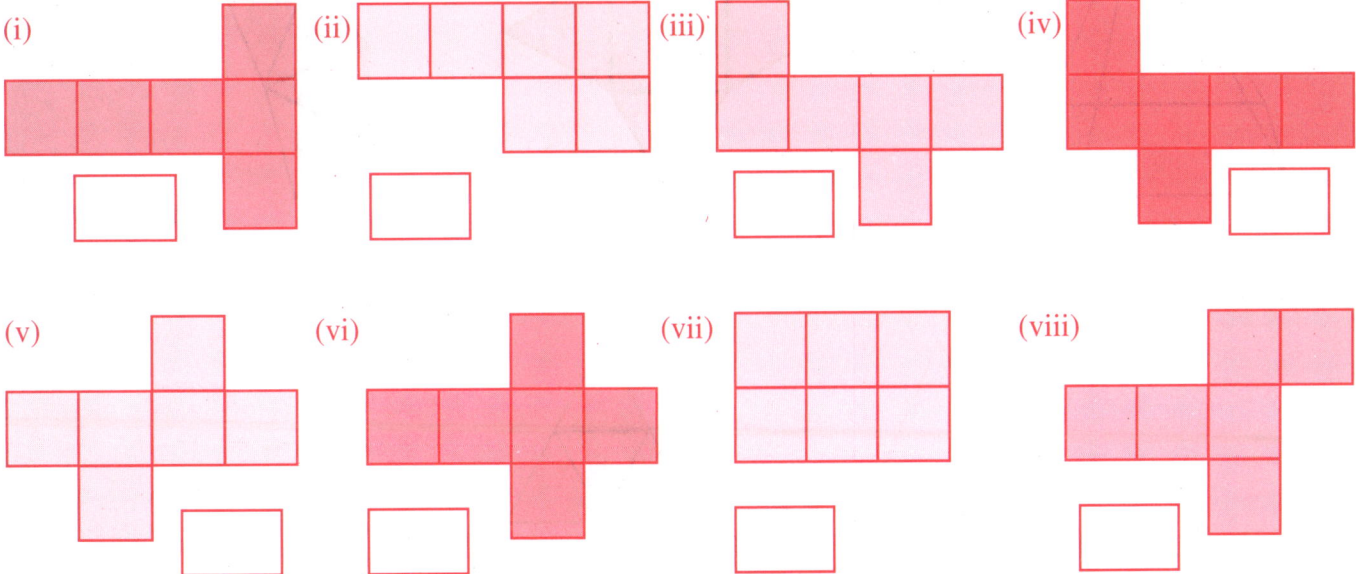

(b) Make a net of a cube different from the nets you have learnt till now.

Cuboid

The cuboid is another solid shape with the same properties as a cube but with two square sides and four rectangular faces. The best examples of cuboids are shoe boxes and suitcases.

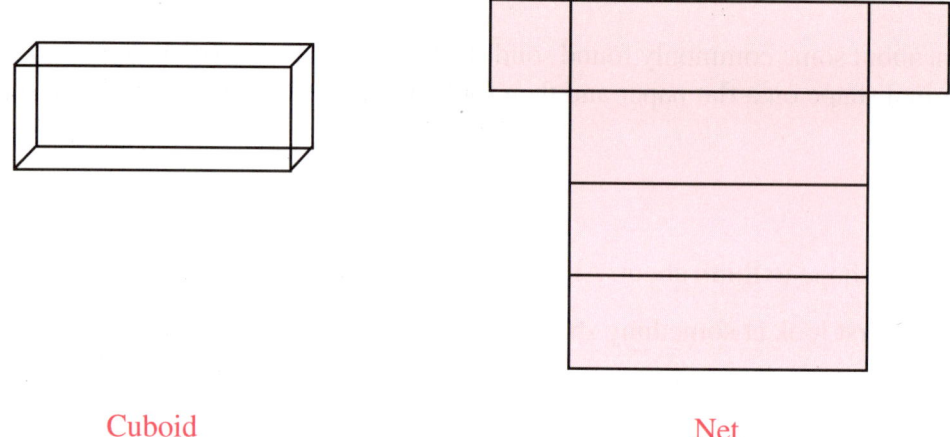

Cuboid   Net

Pyramid

There are two types of pyramids. A square pyramid has one square base and four triangular faces like the one given here.

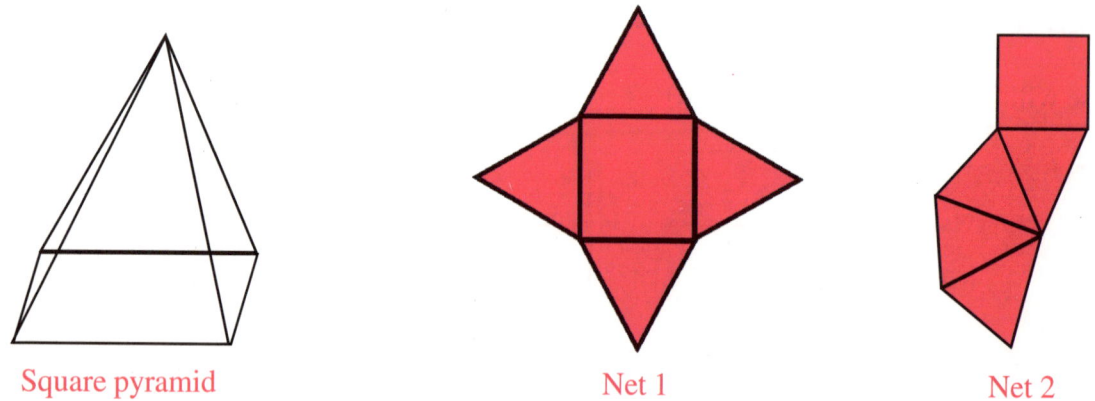

Square pyramid   Net 1   Net 2

A triangular pyramid has four triangular faces. One triangular face makes its base.

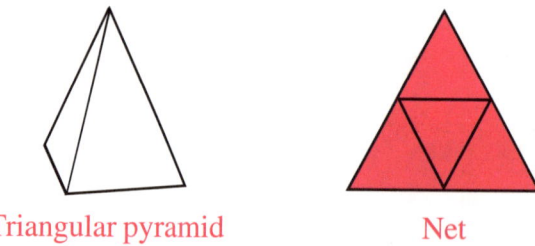

Triangular pyramid   Net

Cone

Cones have curved surfaces as shown below. So, they are not prisms or polyhedra. The point about which the line is rotated is called the vertex and the base of the cone is a circle.

Cone

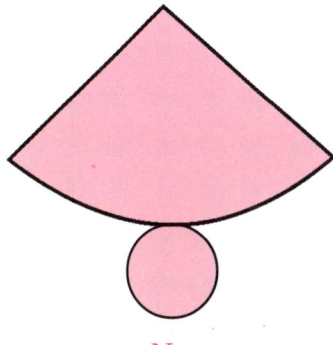
Net

Cylinders

A cylinder is another very common solid shape that we can see in plenty in our environment. Drink cans are a good example.

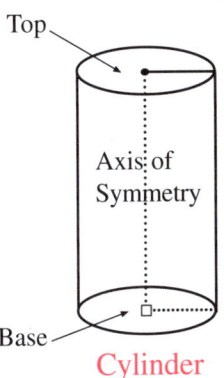
Cylinder

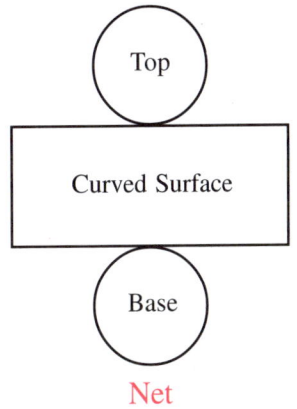
Net

The net of a cylinder consists of three parts.

- One circle forms the base and another circle forms the top.
- A rectangle makes the curved surface.

Exercise 4

(a) Give two examples of each shape from your surroundings.

(i) Cuboid

(ii) Cube

(iii) Cylinder

(iv) Cone

(v) Pyramid

(vi) Triangular pyramid

(b) Write which shape would be formed by using the following nets.

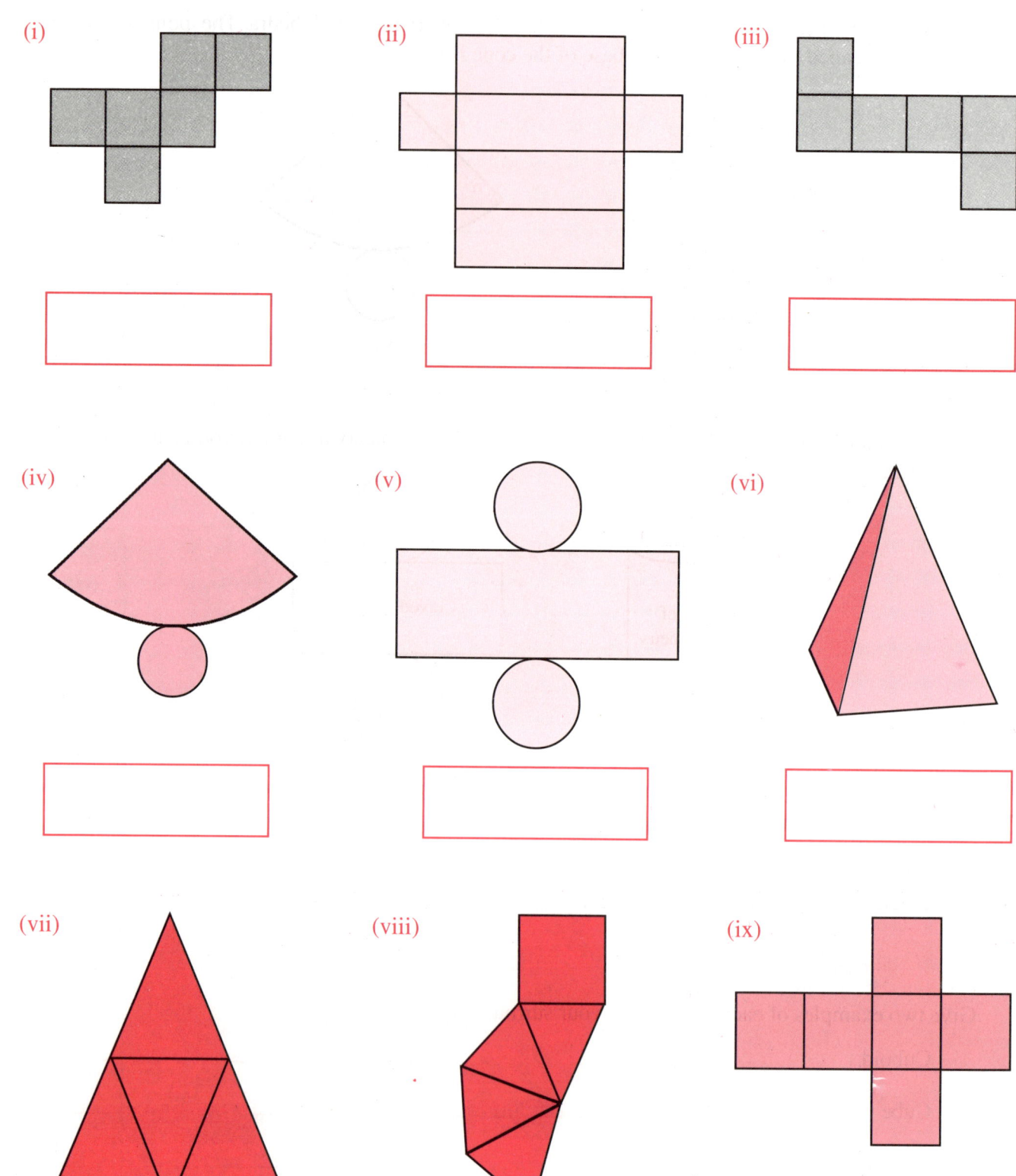

Chapter 19 — Angles

> **You know...**
> - there are several types of angles
> - rays meet to form angles
> - angles are measured by using a protractor.

What do you know about a line, line segment and ray?

I know what a line is.

Line
(a) A line is made up of many points joined together.
(b) A line extends endlessly in both directions.
(c) It has no definite length.
(d) It has no end points.

I know what a line segment is.

Line segment
(a) A line segment is a straight line which has a beginning and an end.
(b) It is a part of a line.
(c) It has two end points.
(d) It has a definite length.

I know what a ray is.

Ray
(a) A ray has a beginning but no end.
(b) It extends endlessly in one direction.

Now look at this figure. $\overrightarrow{OA}$ and $\overrightarrow{OB}$ are two rays meeting at a common point 'O' to form an **angle**.

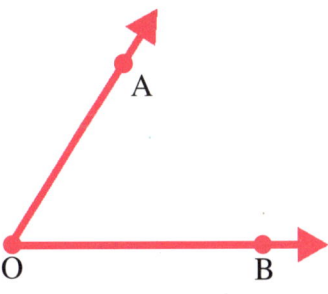

The point 'O' where the angle is formed is known as the vertex of the angle AOB. OA and OB are the arms of the angle AOB. An angle is named after the letter given to the vertex.

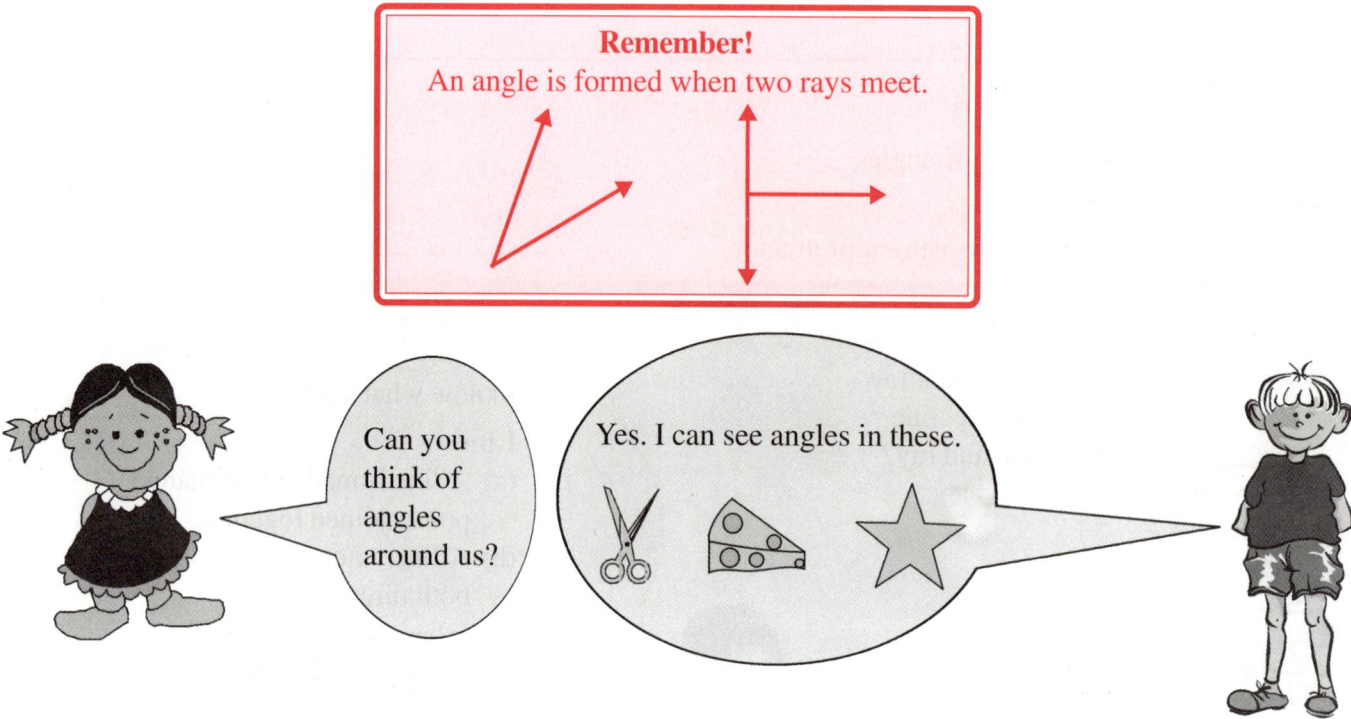

Exercise 1

(a) Name all the possible angles in the following figures.

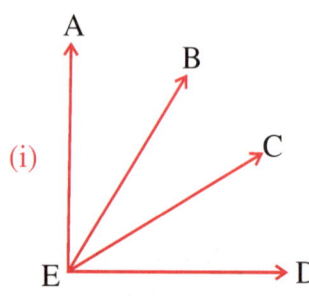 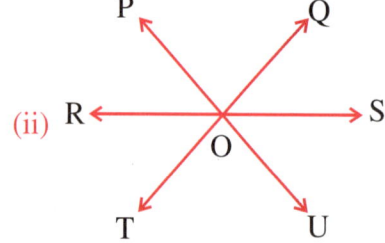 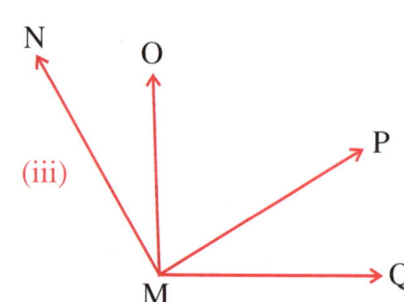

(b) Draw any four objects which show angles.

Exercise 2

Name all the possible angles in the following.

Example

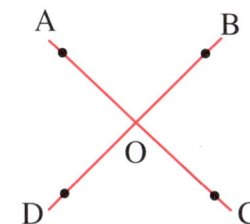

∠AOB ∠AOC ∠BOC ∠DOC ∠AOD

Name the angles.

(a)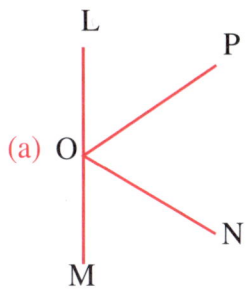

(b)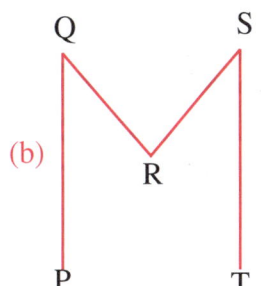

(c)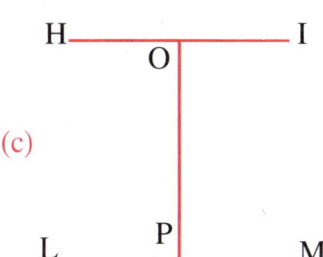

_____   _____   _____

Measuring Angles

How do I measure angles?

To measure angles, use an instrument called a protractor.

It is in the shape of a semicircle.

It has measurements from 0° to 180°.

Degree is the unit used to measure an angle.

A protractor has two sets of numbers written on it, from left to right and right to left. This enables measurement of angles from both sides. If the arm which forms the base line is to the right of the vertex, you measure from the right. If it is to the left of the vertex, you measure from the left. Each single division is called a **degree**.

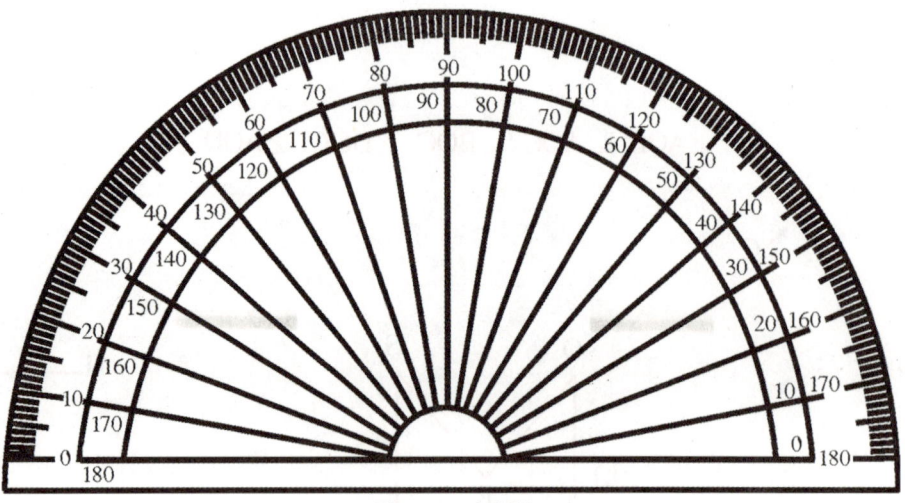

Centre = 90°

Look at this.

Here is how to measure the given angle PQC (in anti-clockwise direction).

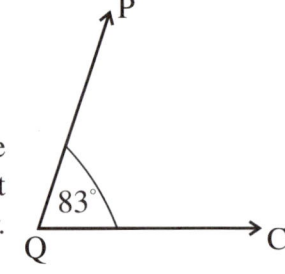

Place the protractor in such a way that the centre of the protractor is exactly on the vertex of the angle PQC. QC is the base line and it is facing the right. So start measuring from C and stop where QP is in line with one of the arms of the protractor. This shows 83°.

Exercise 3

Use a protractor to confirm the measures of the following angles.

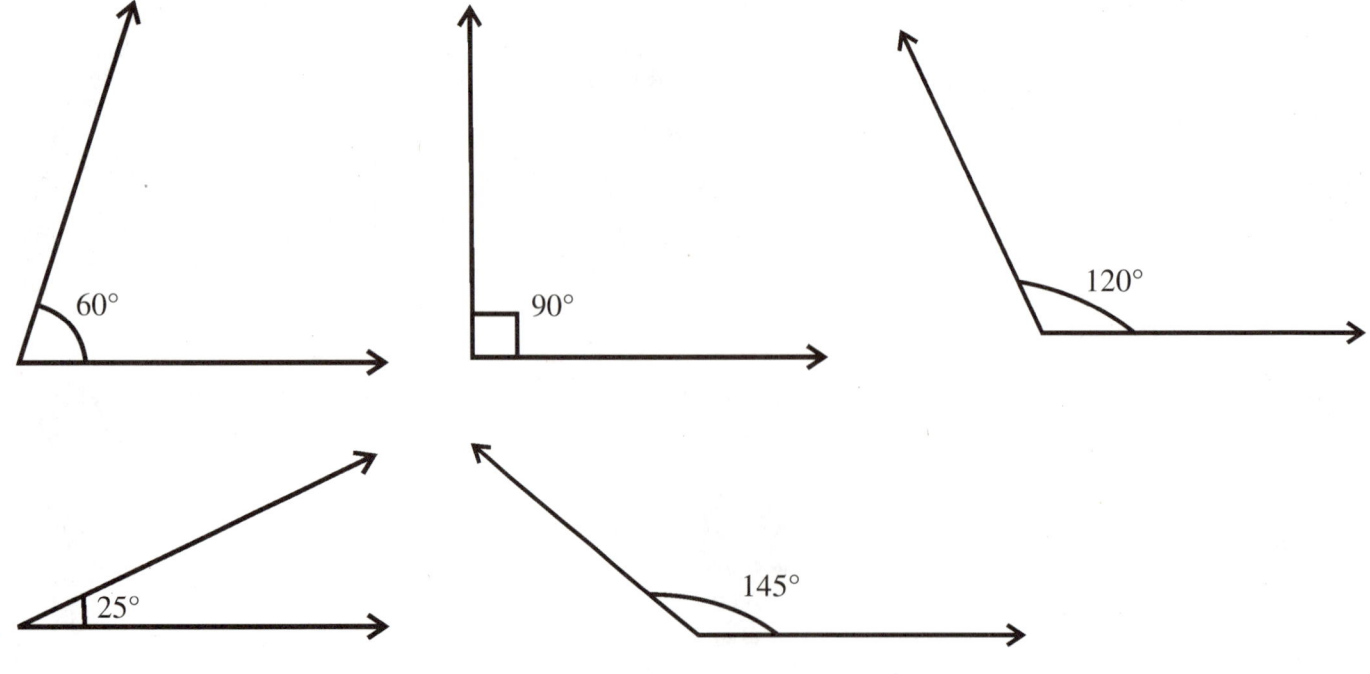

Exercise 4

Measure the following angles by using a protractor.

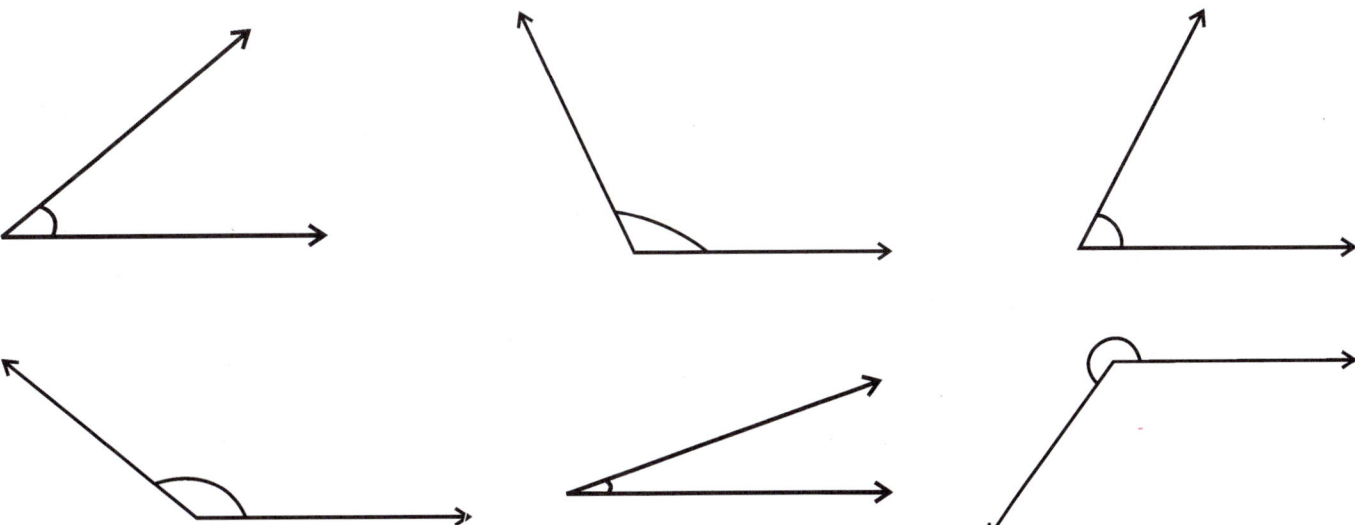

Types of Angles

Angles are of different types. They are named according to the measurement they show.

Acute Angle

An angle which is less than 90° is an acute angle.

Right Angle

An angle that measures exactly 90° is a right angle.

Obtuse Angle

An angle which is more than 90° but less than 180° is an obtuse angle.

Straight Angle

An angle that measures exactly 180° is a straight angle.

Reflex Angle

An angle that measures more than 180° but less than 360° is a reflex angle.

Exercise 5

Draw angles for the following measurements and determine the type of the angles.

(a) 120° (b) 45° (c) 320°

(d) 90° (e) 180° (f) 60°

(g) 110° (h) 20° (i) 240°

Exercise 6

Write True or False for the following statements.

(a) A line has a definite length.

(b) A line segment has two end points.

(c) A line segment and a ray form an angle.

(d) Parallel lines meet at one end.

(e) Angles are measured in degrees.

(f) A pair of compasses is used to draw angles.

(g) There are many types of angles.　　☐

(h) An angle is formed at the vertex.　　☐

(i) A right angle measures exactly 180°.　　☐

(j) An angle of 360° is formed at a point.　　☐

Exercise 7

Colour the right box. The first one has been done.

Angles	Acute	Obtuse	Right	Straight	Reflex
45°	✓				
90°					
120°					
250°					
10°					
180°					
190°					
170°					

Vocabulary Learnt

acute　　　obtuse　　　right　　　straight

reflex　　　angle　　　measure

ray　　　degree　　　definite　　　line segment

protractor　　　extend　　　vertex

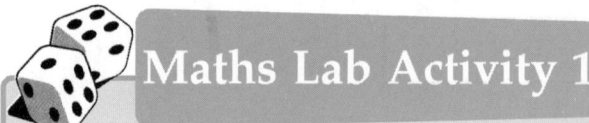

Maths Lab Activity 1

Angle puppet

Materials required

(a) 10 strips of 2 cm x 16 cm per student (b) 6 split pins per student

(c) One head with a neck which is 2 cm wide and 2 cm long for each student

Method (Note for the Teacher)

Ask the students to punch holes at both ends of 6 strips and at only one end in the other strips. Ash them to punch a hole in the neck. Now ask them to join all the pieces together to form a puppet like this.

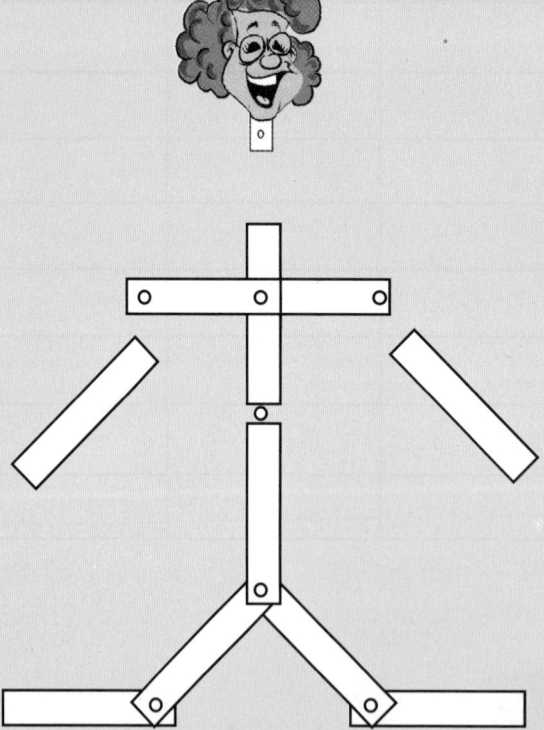

They can paint the face. The puppet can be positioned in different postures and the students can be asked to name all the angles formed by the hands and the legs.

Chapter 20

Triangles

> **You know...**
> - triangle is one of the plane shapes
> - the difference between plane and solid shapes
> - triangles can be of different types
> - triangles have three sides, three vertices and three angles.

You are already familiar with many closed shapes. Triangle is one such closed figure. I am sure you know most of the characteristics of a triangle. Can you write down all that you can remember?

_____

_____

In this chapter, you will learn more about triangles. Triangles can be of different types and sizes, but all of them have only three sides, three corners and three angles. Also, the sum of the three angles will always be 180°, whatever be the type and size of the triangle.

Exercise 1

Look at the following triangles.

(a) 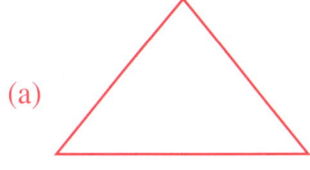　(b) 　(c)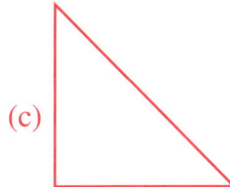

(d) 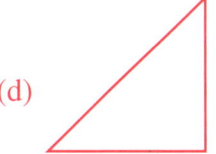　(e) 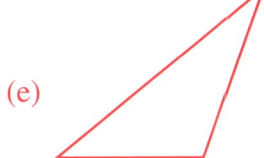　(f)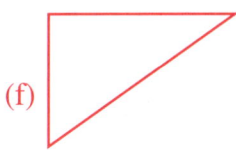

(g) 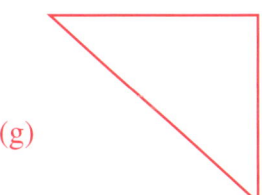　(h) 　(i)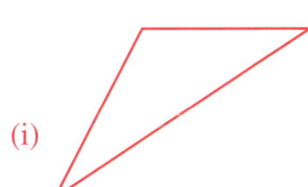

Name the three angles in each of the triangles.

Example

(a) It has three acute angles.

(b) It has two acute angles and one right angle.

(c) _____

(d) _____

(e) _____

(f) _____

(g) _____

(h) _____

(i) _____

Exercise 2

(a)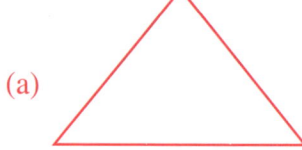

(b)

(c)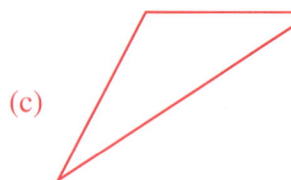

(d)

(e)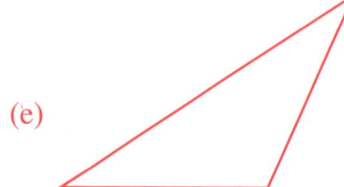

(f)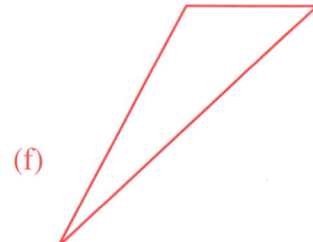

Answer the following questions.

(a) How many triangles have more than one right angle? _____

(b) How many of them have two obtuse angles? _____

(c) How many have one obtuse and one right angle? _____

(d) How many have all angles that are more than 60°? _____

(e) How many have all angles that are less than 60°? _____

Give reasons for your answers to the fourth and fifth questions.

_____

_____

_____

_____

Some important points about triangles that we observe are given below.

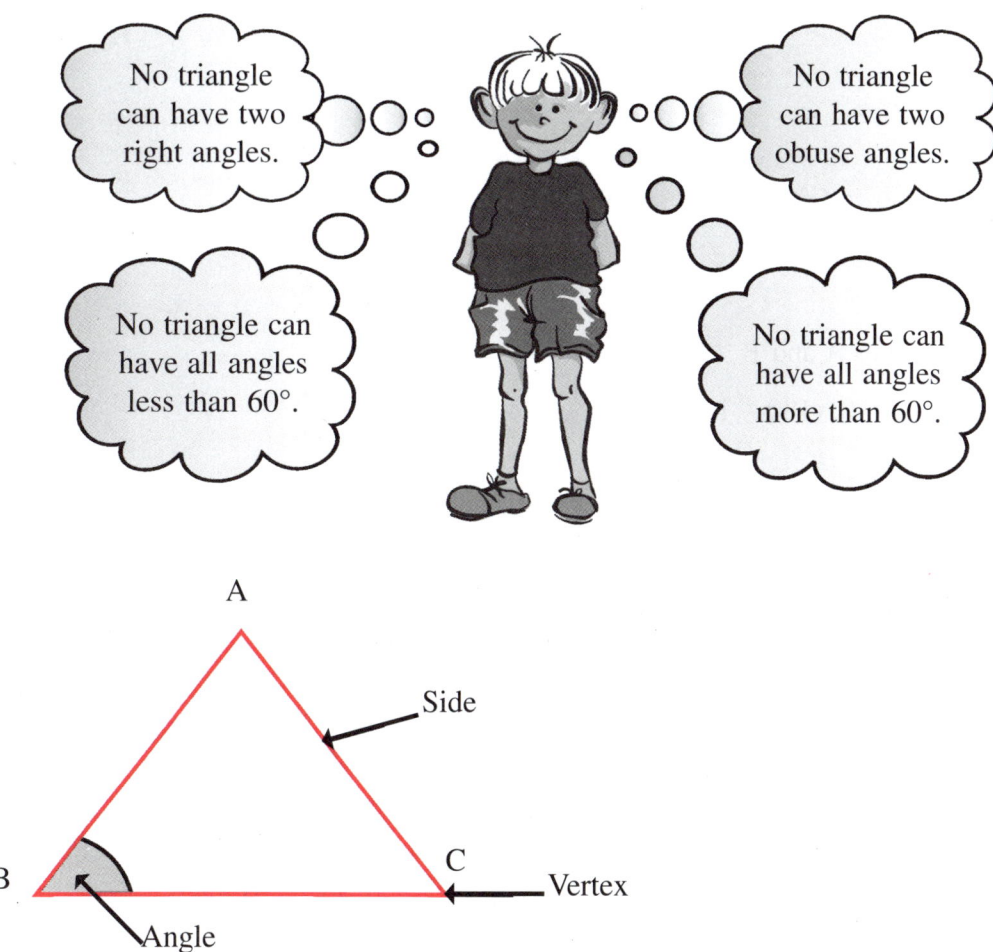

(a) A triangle has three sides. Here, AB, AC and BC are the sides.

(b) A triangle has three vertices. A, B and C are the vertices.

(c) A triangle has three angles. ABC, ACB and BAC are the three angles.
    (Angles are always formed at the vertex.)

Angles of a Triangle

As explained in the previous chapter, the angle of a triangle is measured by using a tool called a protractor.

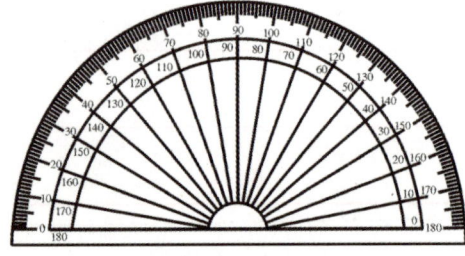

A protractor has markings from 0° to 180° marked from either side in order to enable the measurement of an angle from both sides.

You know that the sum of the three angles of any triangle is equal to 180°. If the measures of two angles are given, how will you find the measure of the third angle?

Look at this.

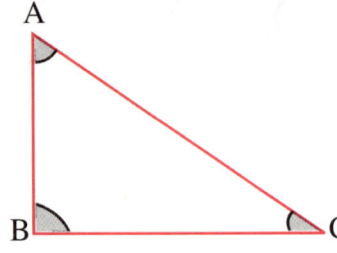

∠A = 45°   ∠B = 90°   Find ∠C?

Step 1: Add the measures of angles A and B. (45 + 90 = 135).

Step 2: Subtract their total from 180. (180 – 135 = 45).

Therefore, angle C = 45°.

Exercise 3

Look at the triangles given below carefully to find the measure of the third angle.

(a)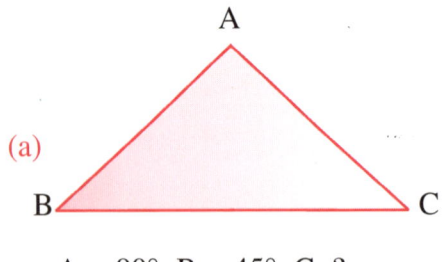

A = 90°, B = 45°, C=?

(b)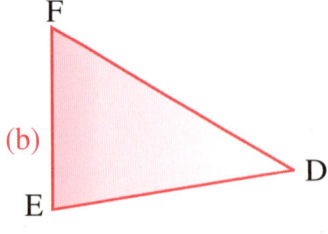

D = 45°, E = 85°, F=?

(c)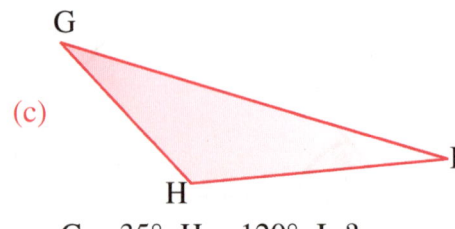

G = 35°, H = 120°, I=?

(d)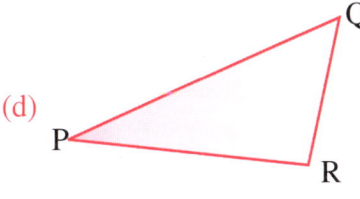
P = 42°, R = 90°, Q=?

(e)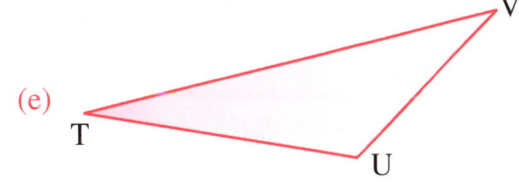
V = 28°, U = 110°, T=?

Exercise 4

Find the third angle without using diagrams.

(a) 25°, 43° (b) 90°, 25° (c) 51°, 95°

(d) 65°, 90° (e) 85°, 15° (f) 120°, 20°

(g) 110°, 30° (h) 45°, 45° (i) 60°, 60°

Exercise 5

Measure the three angles of the following triangles and check if they add up to 180°.

(a) 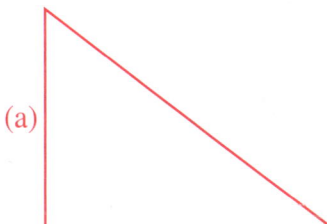 (b) 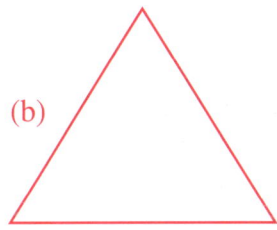 (c)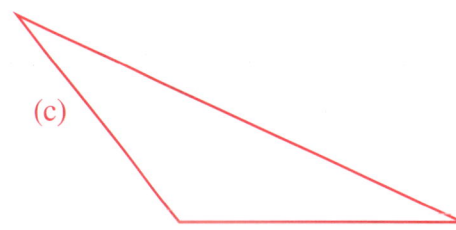

(d) (e)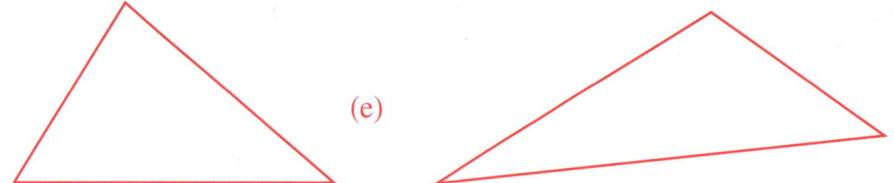

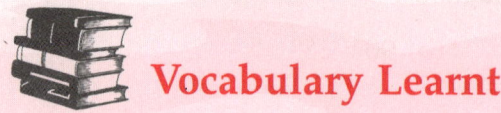
Vocabulary Learnt

measure　　　　　　　　sum　　　　　　　　vertex

closed figure　　　　　　degree

 ## Maths Lab Activity 1

Materials required

(a) Any type of reasonably big (with sides of at least 8 cms) triangle, cut out of chart paper.

(b) Sketch pens　　　(c) Ruler　　　(d) Pencil and eraser

Method (Note for the Teacher)

Ask the students to make two triangles and check the sum of the angles (180°) by both the methods given below. You can explain the steps or dictate them.

| Method 1 |

Step 1: Mark the three angles of the triangle.

Step 2: Cut the triangle into three parts, using straight lines but make sure that there is one angle in each part.

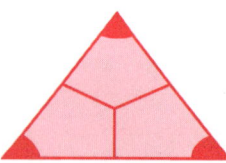

Step 3: Draw a straight line on a chart paper, mark a point in the centre and mark an angle around the point. You already know that a straight line is equal to 180°. 	**Step 4:** Place the three cut parts of the triangle on the straight line, like a puzzle, without leaving gaps. 

Do you notice that when the three pieces are placed together, the angles add to a straight line which is equal to 180°?

Method 2

Step 1: Mark the three angles of the triangle. 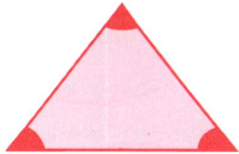	**Step 2:** Find the mid point of the two side lines and join them. 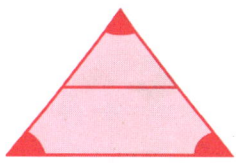
Step 3: Drop a perpendicular from either end on to the base line. 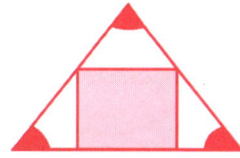	**Step 4:** Fold along the three lines backwards and turn the paper. This is how it will look. 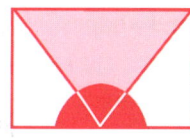

Do you notice that when the three angles are placed together, they form a semicircle which is equal to 180°?

Chapter 21 — Circles

> **You know...**
> - Geometry is a branch of Mathematics
> - shapes form an important part of Geometry
> - how to identify both plane and solid shapes through their individual attributes
> - how to identify and draw the basic shapes.

Can you colour all the circles in the figures given below?

A *circle* is a plane shape that is a little different from other shapes. A circle has no sides or corners like the square, rectangle or triangle. It is a set of points that are equidistant from a given point joined together. This point is called the *centre*. The distance from the centre to anywhere on the circle will be the same.

We use a special instrument called the compass to draw a perfect circle.

Compass

(a) Fix a pencil with a sharp point into the arm and tighten the screw.

(b) Mark a point (label it with a capital letter) on a sheet of paper.

(c) Open the two arms of the compass as required and fix the sharp end of the compass on the marked centre.

(d) By holding the top of the compass firmly and moving the arm holding the pencil slowly, start drawing a line until it comes back to the starting place and you will get a circle.

If you want to draw or mark huge circles in an open field to organise a game you can use the following method.

Take a piece of rope. Fix one end of if to the ground firmly with a nail. Attach another nail or a long marker at the other end. Holding the rope tight, keep moving the marker on the ground, thus making an impression, until you come back to the starting point. You will find the shape of a circle marked on the ground. Now you may put chalk powder or colour powder over the marking to make it prominent. You will notice that the distance from the centre of the circle to any point on the path is the same.

Centre

The fixed point 'O' at the middle of the circle is called its centre.

Circumference

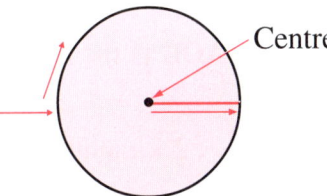

The line which makes the boundary of the circle is called the circumference.

Measuring Circumference

The following activity can be used to measure the circumference of a circle.

Cut a circle from a cardboard and mark a point at any place along the circumference. Draw a line segment on a sheet of paper. Roll the circle along the line segment. Make sure the point you have marked on the circle is your starting point. Roll the circle on till you come back to the starting point and mark the point on the segment. Now, take a ruler and measure the length of the line. You get the circumference of the circle. You can repeat the same exercise with circles of different sizes to find the circumference.

If you measure the diameter of these circles and compare them with their circumferences, you will notice that the circumference is 3 times and a little more than the diameter. This ratio is called pi (Π) and it cannot be measured accurately. Its value is taken as 3.142. The circumference of any circle will be 3.142 times the diameter of that circle.

Find out the circumference of some circular objects around you.

Circular objects	Circumference (Use the length of a thread.)
(a) Top of a tumbler	
(b)	
(c)	
(d)	

Radius

The line joining the centre to any point on the circumference of a circle is called a radius. In the figure given below, OA, OB and OC are all radii. (Plural of radius is radii.) Two circles are said to be equal if their radii are equal.

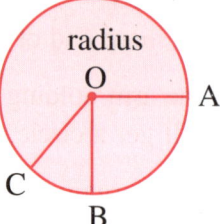

Diameter

The diameter is the line joining two points on the circumference and passing through the centre.

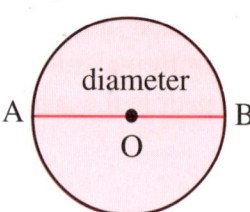

The line AOB is the diameter of the circle. The length of the diameter is equal to twice the length of the radius.

Diameter = 2 × radius.

Semicircle

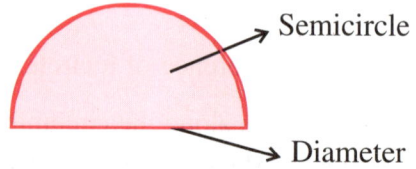

A diameter divides a circle into two halves. Each half is a semicircle.

Arc

A part of the circumference of the circle is called an arc of the circle. Here, $\overarc{AB}$ is the smaller arc while $\overarc{BA}$ is the greater arc.

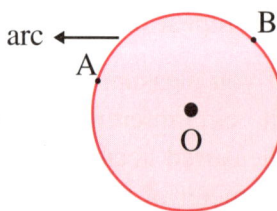

Chord

The line joining any two points on the circumference of a circle is called a *chord* of the circle.

Name all the chords in the following figure.

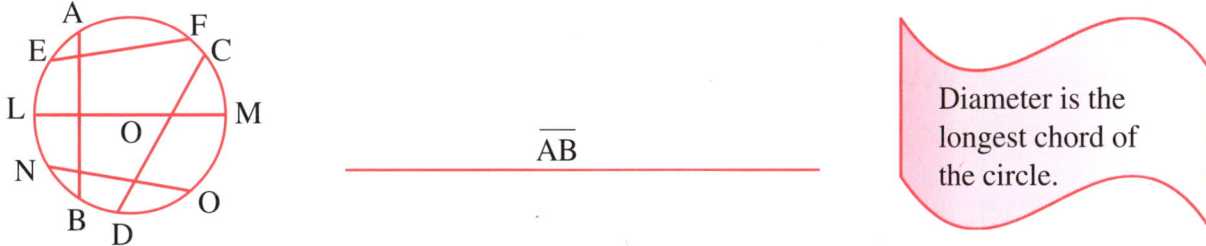

$\overline{AB}$

Diameter is the longest chord of the circle.

Exercise 1

Look at the following circles carefully and complete the table given below.

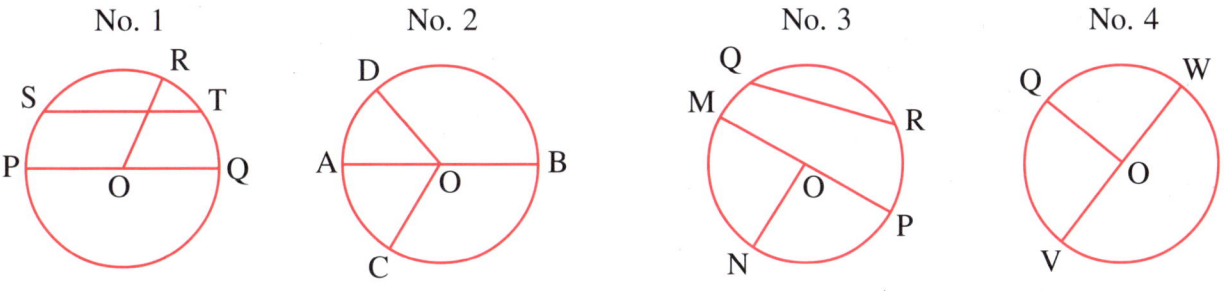

Circle no.	Radius/radii	Diameter	Chord

Sector

The part or portion of the circle within 2 radii is called a *sector*. In the given figure, 2 radii, OP and OQ, divide the circle into a minor sector and a major sector.

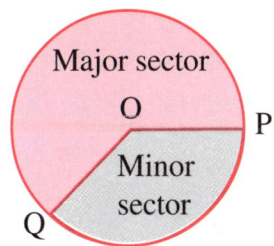

Segment

A chord divides the circle into a major segment and a minor segment.

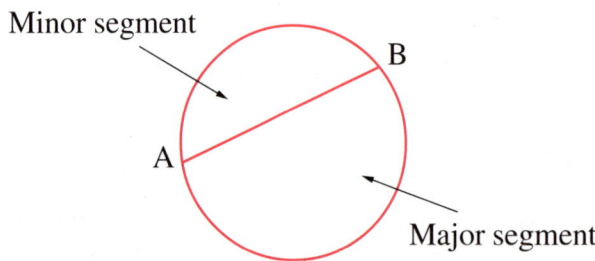

Exercise 2

Look at the circle given below and answer the questions.

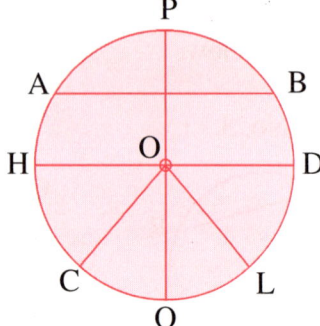

(a) What is O?　　　　　(b) What is HD?　　　　　(c) What is HOC?

_____　　　　　_____　　　　　_____

(d) What is OP?　　　　　(e) What is $\overline{AB}$?　　　　　(f) What is $\overparen{HA}$?

_____　　　　　_____　　　　　_____

(g) What is $\overparen{HPD}$?　　　　(h) What is $\overparen{APB}$?　　　　(i) What is OC?

_____　　　　　_____　　　　　_____

Exercise 3

Write T for True and F for False.

(a) The diameter is the longest chord.

(b) The diameter is two times the circumference.

(c) A circle can have any number of diameters. ☐

(d) What perimeter is to a square, circumference is to a circle. ☐

(e) Radius is two times the diameter. ☐

(f) A diameter passes through the centre. ☐

(g) An arc is a part of the circumference. ☐

(h) A circle has no sides and no corners. ☐

(i) Many lines put together form a circle. ☐

(j) All semicircles are arcs. ☐

Drawing Circles of Various Radii

You should know the radius to be able to draw a circle.

Example   To draw a circle with radius 5 cm.

Step 1: Insert a sharp pencil into the compass.

Step 2: Using the compass, measure 5 cm on a ruler.

Step 3: Mark a point O on the notebook.

Step 4: Place the sharp end of the compass on point 'O'.

Step 5: Hold the top of the compass firmly and turn it around slowly, touching the pencil on the paper, till it comes back to the starting point.

Step 6: Your circle is ready.

You can draw circles of different radii by using this method.

Exercise 4

Draw circles with the following radii. Mark the centre, the radius and the diameter.

(a) 1.5 cm
(b) 2 cm
(c) 1.6 cm

(d) 1.8 cm
(e) 2.2 cm
(f) 2.5 cm

(g) 3 cm
(h) 3.3 cm
(i) 3.5 cm

(j) 3.4 cm
(k) 4 cm

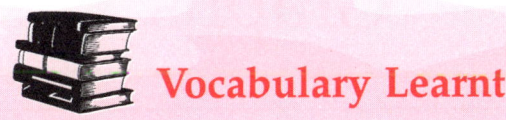

Vocabulary Learnt

boundary   diameter   circumference

segment   chord   sector   radius/radii

arc

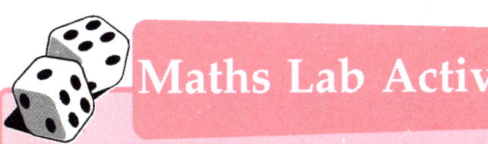

Maths Lab Activity 1

Materials required

(a) Flash cards with words that describe different parts of a circle (diameter, radius, chord, etc.)

(b) Cards with descriptions about each of the parts.

Method (Note for the Teacher)

Divide the students into three groups. Give the flash cards with words to one group and the cards with descriptions to the other group. Ask one person from the first group to show a card (say diameter). One person from the second group should show the card that describes the diameter, that is, it is a line that runs from one end to the other end of the circle through the centre. Then, a student from the third group should go up to the board and draw a circle and its diameter. Continue the game till all the parts have been called out. If time permits, or on another day, they could exchange the cards and play again. Some cards are given below. There can be more cards having same definitions with a slight change in language.

The boundary of a circle	chord	The chord divides the circle into two of these	diameter
sector	A part of a circle	circumference	The part of a circle contained within two radii
The line that passes from one end of the circle to the other, through the centre	centre	The line from the centre to anywhere on the circumference	arc
radius	A line joining any two points on a circle, that is other than the diameter.	segment	The point from where a circle is drawn

Chapter 22

Graphs

> **You know...**
> - the four types of graphs
> - how to construct graphs
> - how to interpret graphs.

Graphs are of different kinds. They are used to show data or information, usually using numbers, pictures or symbols.

Can you think of all the things you need to make a graph?

List them down.

_____

_____

_____

Steps to follow when you want to make a graph.

Step 1: Read and gather information.

Step 2: Decide the variables to be shown on the two axes.

Step 3: Choose a suitable key, where necessary, so that you can represent all the numbers involved in the graph.

Step 4: Decide which type of graph will be the most suitable for the given information.

Once you are ready with all these, it is very easy to draw a graph. Graphs help the reader to gather all the information that is required. Given below are examples of different kinds of graphs one can make.

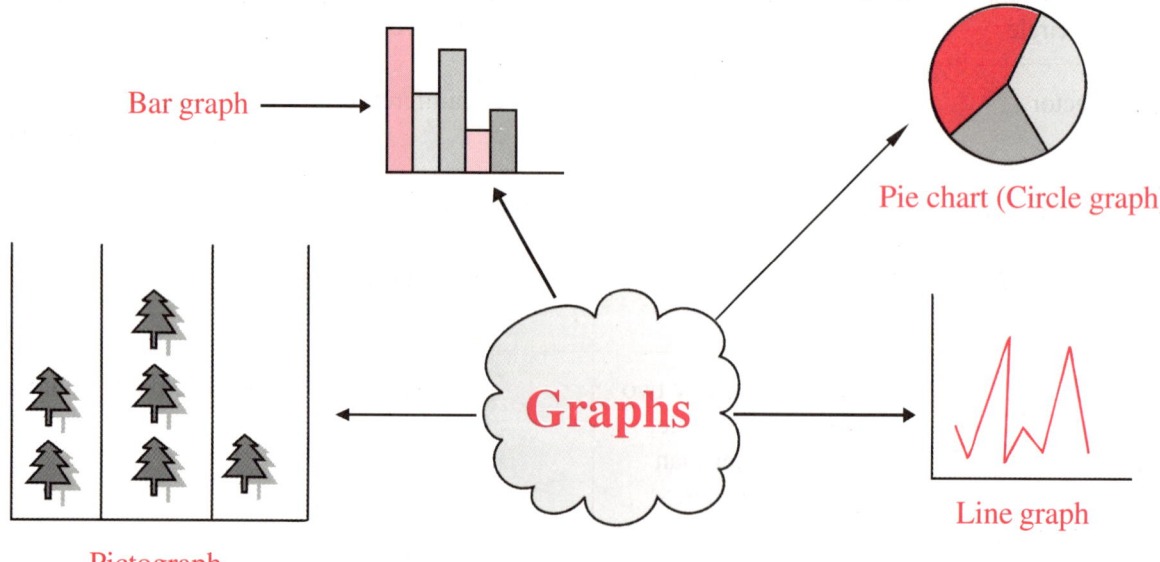

Grids

Many graphs show information on grids also. A grid is made up of many horizontal and vertical lines that intersect. The pattern or the design is created on this grid using the coordinates. The horizontal line at the bottom is called the x axis and the vertical line to the extreme left is called the y axis. Their meeting point should be marked as 'O'. To locate or find points on the grid, you need to know the numbers or letters that you are going to mark on the grid. They are called the ordered pair. You should take the number or letter from the horizontal axis first and then from the vertical axis. All the points located on the same graph are called coordinates.

Bar Graph

A lot of information can be shown with the help of a bar graph.

Exercise 1

Here is your chance to make a bar graph. Read the information given here carefully and then draw the graph.

A primary school staged a play to raise funds for its institution. Each class was asked to sell tickets. Here is the number of tickets sold by each class.

        Class 1 – 120 tickets   Class 4 – 204 tickets

        Class 2 – 185 tickets   Class 5 – 105 tickets

        Class 3 – 83 tickets

Answer the following questions.

(a) What is the graph about?   _____

(b) What will you represent in the x axis?   _____

(c) What will you represent in the y axis?   _____

(d) How will you divide the y axis to show the numbers?   _____

(e) Do you need a key to show the number of tickets sold?   _____

Now, draw the bar graph in the space provided and colour it.

Converting Data into a Table

The weights (in kg) of 15 students in a class are given below.

38   35   37   38   36   39   42   43   40   36   35   37   38   39   44

The data given above can be made more organised and informative.

Weight (kg)	35	36	37	38	39	40	41	42	43	44
Frequency	2	2	2	3	2	1	0	1	1	1

This data tells us how many students have 35 kg weight, 36 kg weight and so on.

Pictograph

Unlike bar graphs, pictographs require symbols or pictures to show the information. So your pictograph should be simple.

Exercise 2

Make a pictograph to show the following information.

Sam and his friends visited his father's farm one day. There, they saw 8 mangoes, 6 oranges, 7 guavas, 10 coconuts, 3 jack fruits and 7 papayas.

Answer the following questions.

(a) What is the graph about? _____

(b) What will the x axis represent? _____

(c) What will the y axis represent? _____

(d) What symbols will you use? _____

(e) What is the key to represent all the trees? _____

Now make the pictograph to show the given information.

Line Graph

Line graphs are very simple to draw. A line graph is usually used to show gradual changes or changes that take place over a period of time.

Exercise 3

Read the information given below carefully and make a line graph.

Balu left from Chennai to Krishnagiri (a distance of 200 km) by car, on a Sunday morning at 6:00 a.m. In the first hour, he covered 50 km, in the second hour, he covered 35 km, in the third hour, he covered 32 km, in the fourth hour, again he picked up some speed and covered 48 km and, in the last hour, he drove 35 km.

Answer the following questions.

(a) What is the graph about? _____

(b) What will the x axis represent? _____

(c) What will the y axis represent? _____

(d) What is your key going to show? _____

Now draw the line graph.

Pie Chart or Circle Graph

Pie chart or a circle graph is slightly different because a circle is 'divided into parts' to show the information. The parts will vary in size according to the information presented.

Exercise 4

It was sports day in Ramu's school. The students of his class were allowed to choose any one game out of the six games announced. 33% of the students chose athletics, 21% of the students chose high jump, 18% chose long jump, 12% chose short put, 10% chose 100 m race and 6% of the students chose javelin throw. Represent the above information on a circle graph.

Answer the following questions.

(a) What is the graph about? _____

(b) How many parts are required in all in the graph? _____

(c) How many games have to be presented in the graph? _____

(d) Which is the highest chosen game? _____

(e) Which is the least chosen game? _____

(f) Why do you think many students did not opt for javelin throw? _____

(g) If you were a part of this school, which game would you have chosen? Why? _____

Now make your graph in the given circle.

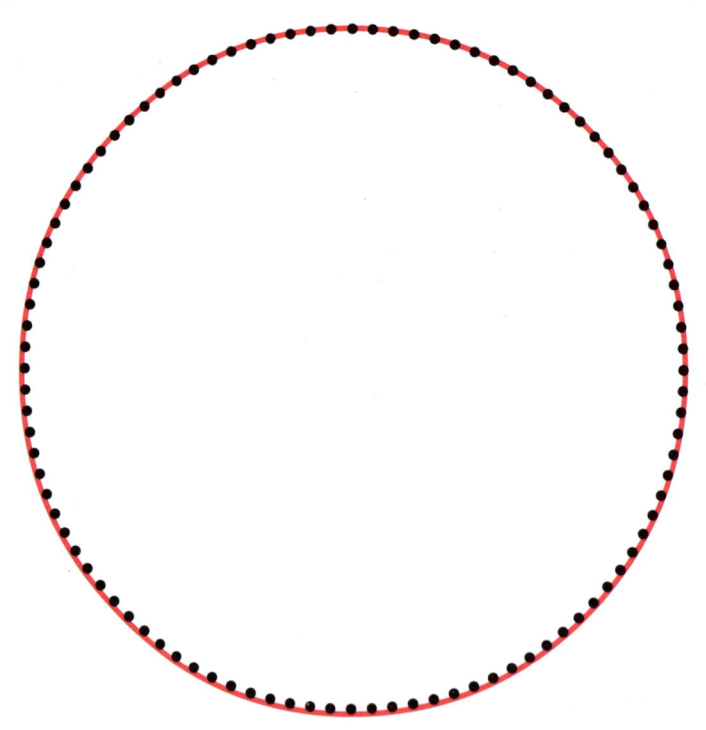

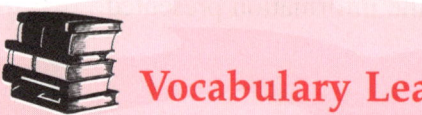

Vocabulary Learnt

ordered pair   pie   axis/axes

grid   locate

Maths Lab Activity 1

Materials Required

(a) Worksheets having incomplete figures and coordinates (b) Pencil

Method (Note for the Teacher)

Distribute worksheets to all the students. Ask them to mark all the coordinates and complete the figures. Students can be asked to make such worksheets. They can exchange and work on some other day.

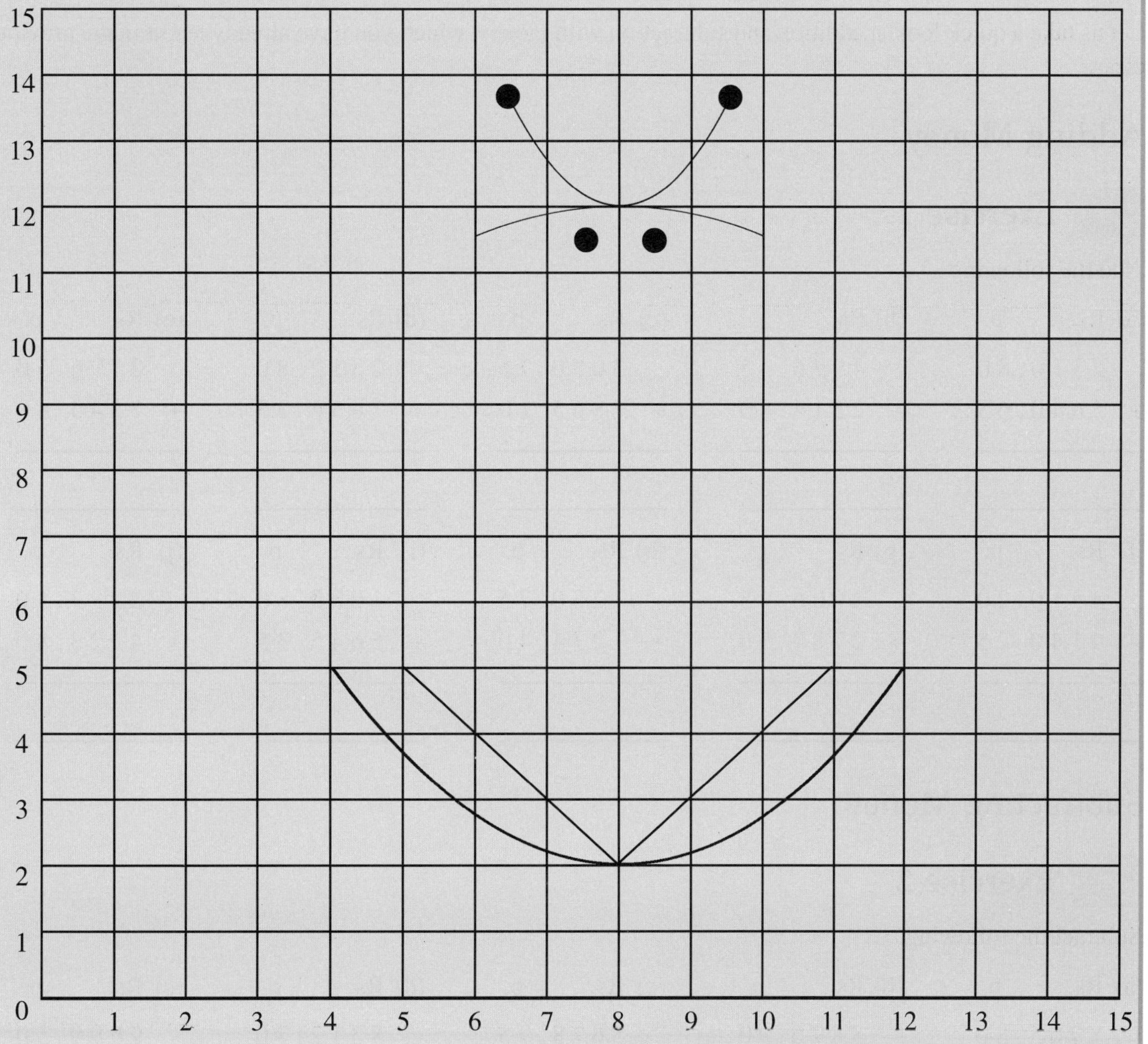

(6,11), (5,10), (4,9), (3,7), (2,5), (2,2), (5,5), (6,7), (8,11),
(10,7), (11,5), (14,2), (14,5), (13,7) (12,9), (11,10), (10,11),

Chapter 23

Money

> **You know…**
> - why people need money
> - conversions by using different denominations and values
> - how to save money
> - how to add or subtract money.

Let us take a quick look at addition and subtraction with money, which you have already learnt in the previous class.

Adding Money

Exercise 1

Add the following.

	(a) Rs. p.	(b) Rs. p.	(c) Rs. p.	(d) Rs. p.	(e) Rs. p.
	2310.80	4976.45	3080.75	2312.80	2796.50
	+ 5640.65	+ 2314.80	+ 7865.10	+ 7656.35	+ 7543.80

	(f) Rs. p.	(g) Rs. p.	(h) Rs. p.	(i) Rs. p.	(j) Rs. p.
	4510.20	2006.45	1230.75	1080.80	2223.50
	+ 4140.25	+ 2789.50	+ 1234.40	+ 5645.35	+ 4123.80

Subtracting Money

Exercise 2

Subtract the following.

	(a) Rs. p.	(b) Rs. p.	(c) Rs. p.	(d) Rs. p.	(e) Rs. p.
	8765.80	8876.90	5678.75	8312.70	9999.50
	− 3140.65	− 2214.10	− 1234.10	− 1656.35	− 3451.80

(f) Rs. p.	(g) Rs. p.	(h) Rs. p.	(i) Rs. p.	(j) Rs. p.
5760.80	8768.55	4580.75	7546.90	5667.50
− 3123.45	− 1235.10	− 2711.20	− 1122.25	− 2001.30

Word Attack

(a) You save Rs. 12.00 in January, Rs. 24.00 in February, Rs. 36.00 in March and so on. How much money would you save in December if you maintain this pattern?

(b) If you save Rs. 2.00 in January, Rs. 4.00 in February, Rs. 8.00 in March, Rs. 16.00 in April and so on, how much money would you save in one year if you maintain this pattern?

(c) Ram wanted money for his weekly expenses. His father gave him two choices of getting it – either once a week or daily. He said he would either pay him Rs. 325 a week or pay him daily in the following manner – Rs. 5 on Monday, Rs. 10 on Tuesday, Rs. 20 on Wednesday, Rs. 40 on Thursday and so on, till Sunday. Which option do you think he should choose to get more money? How much more would he get?

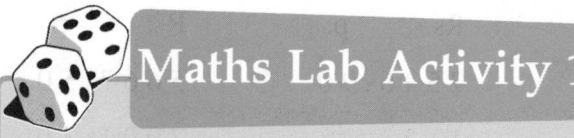

Maths Lab Activity 1

Materials required

(a) Problems as given below (b) Pencil (c) Notebook

Method (Note for the Teacher)

Give a sheet having five problems, as shown below, to each student. Ask them to solve all the problems. Help them wherever necessary.

Problem 1

What is the cost of the doll?

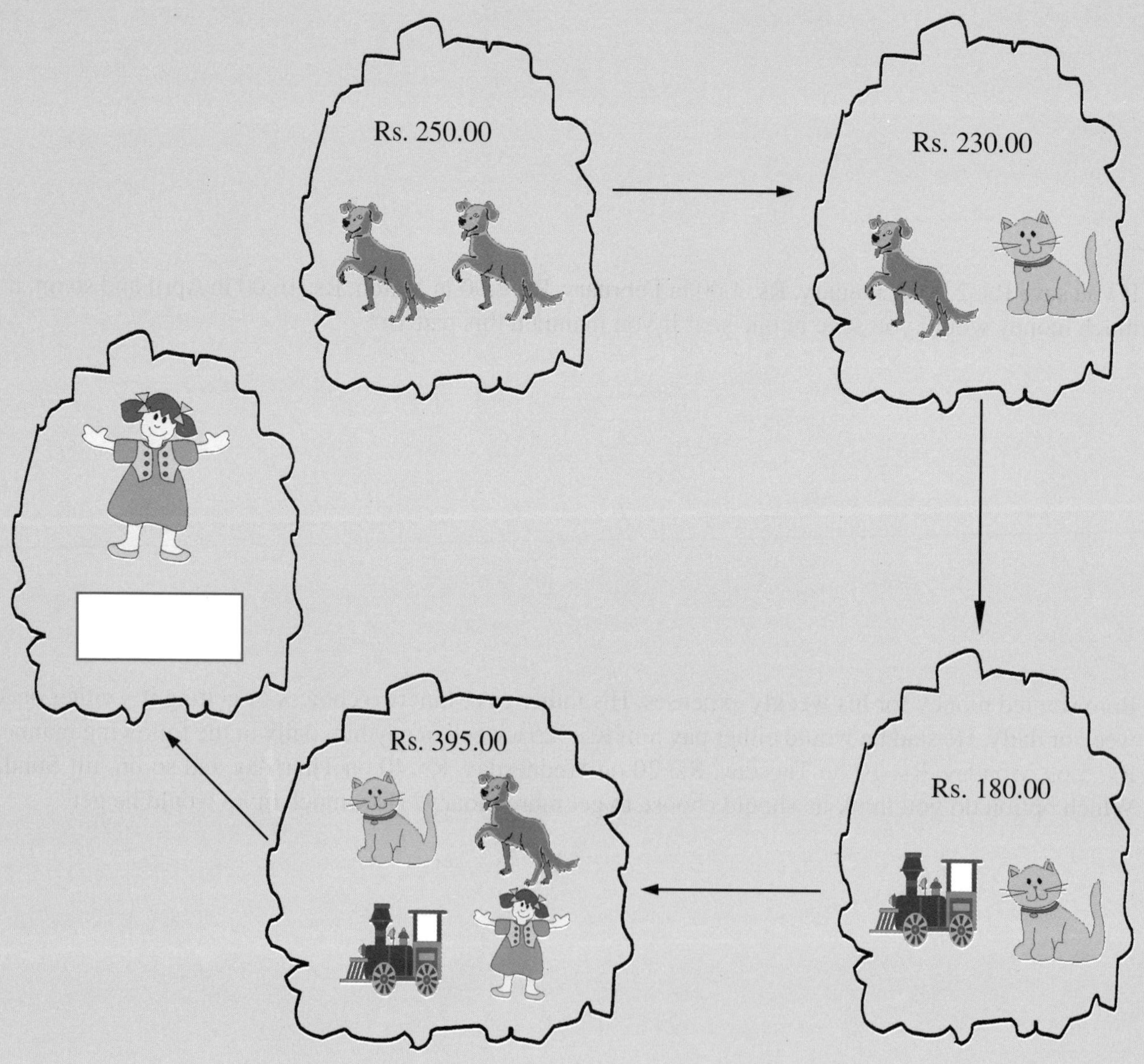

Rs. 250.00 (two dogs)

Rs. 230.00 (dog and cat)

Rs. 180.00 (train and cat)

Rs. 395.00 (cat, dog, train and doll)

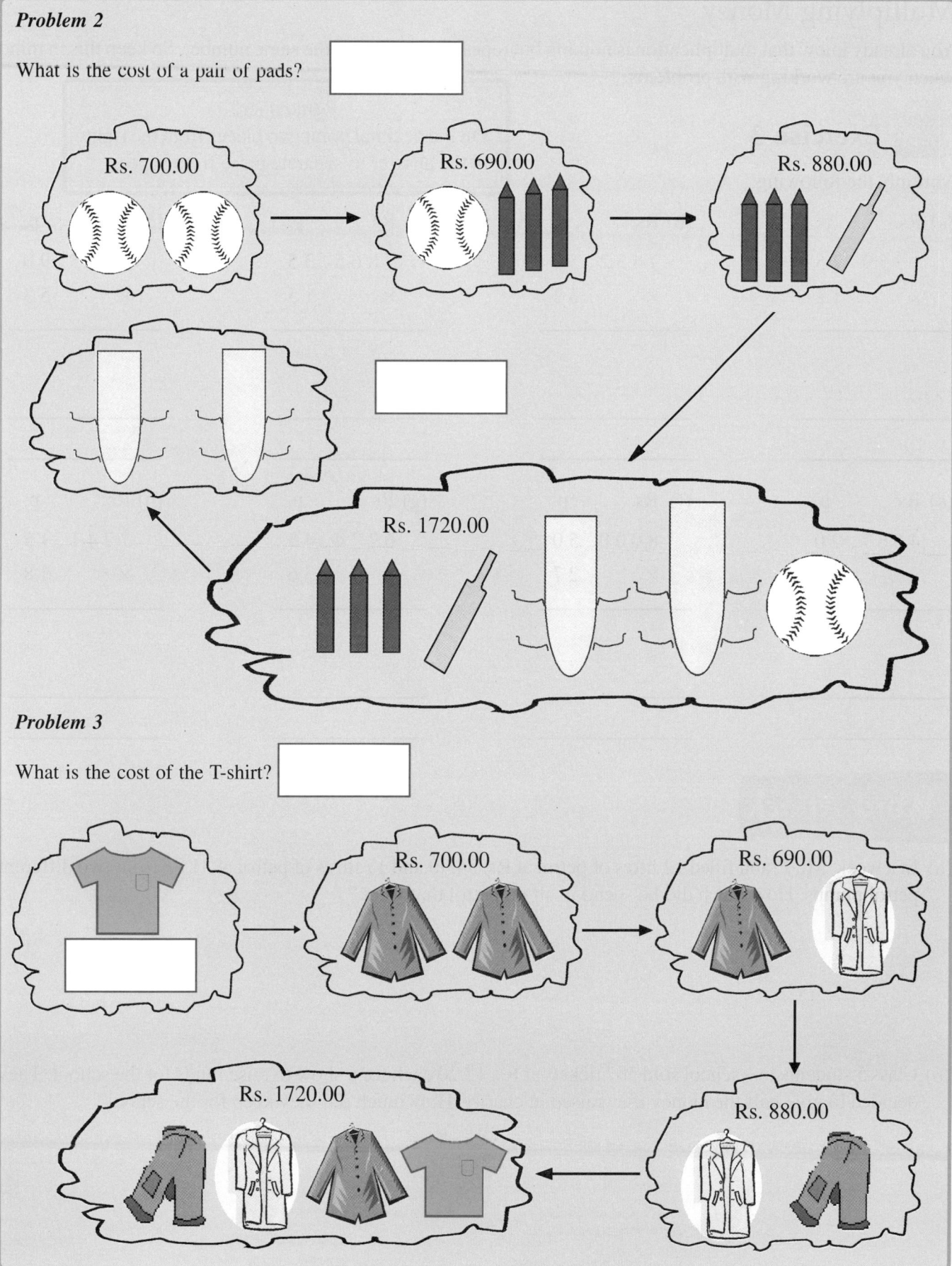

Multiplying Money

You already know that multiplication is nothing but repeated addition of the same number. So keep this in mind when you are working with problems.

Exercise 3

Remember!
Put the decimal point two places from the right in the answer to separate paise from rupees.

Multiply the following.

(a) Rs.   p.
  1 7 5 9 . 7 5
×   1 2
_____

(b) Rs.   p.
  7 4 3 2 . 5 0
×   3 2
_____

(c) Rs.   p.
  7 8 6 5 . 3 5
×   1 5
_____

(d) Rs.   p.
  1 0 2 3 . 9 0
×   5 3
_____

(e) Rs.   p.
  4 5 6 7 . 2 0
×   5 6
_____

(f) Rs.   p.
  8 0 0 0 . 5 0
×   2 7
_____

(g) Rs.   p.
  6 2 2 4 . 4 5
×   3 6
_____

(h) Rs.   p.
  7 7 4 1 . 1 5
×   1 8
_____

Word Attack

(a) In a week, Mr. Prabu filled 12 litres of petrol at Rs. 34.90 and 17 litres of petrol at 31.85 from two different petrol pumps. How much did he spend in all on petrol that week?

(b) Class 5 students in a school sold 567 tickets at Rs. 12.20 each for a show to raise funds for the school. They decided to give half the money they raised in charity. How much did they keep for the school?

(c) Jeeva wanted to buy beads of three different colours to make a necklace for her mother as a surprise birthday gift. She selected three kinds of beads in the store. The purple bead was 25 p each, the yellow bead was 50 p each and the red bead was 75 p each. She wanted to spend Rs. 9.00. How many maximum beads do you think she could have bought with her money? How many beads of each kind did she buy?

(d) Tobby has Rs. 3455.00 with him. He buys two chairs for Rs. 735.25 each and two corner tables for Rs. 516.00 each. How much did he spend? How much money was he left with?

Dividing Money

You already know that division is repeated subtraction of the same number. So keep this in mind when you are working with problems.

> **Remember!**
> Put the decimal point two places from the right in the answer to separate paise from rupees.

Exercise 4

Divide the following.

(a) Rs. 5670.50 ÷ 25

(b) Rs. 9976.50 ÷ 9

(c) Rs. 6096.40 ÷ 8

(d) Rs. 5863.00 ÷ 11

(e) Rs. 3874.50 ÷ 15

(f) Rs. 11080.80 ÷ 19

Word Attack

(a) Mr. Maran was given Rs. 5,67,890 when he retired from service. He kept Rs. 1,25,600.00 for himself and distributed the rest among his three sons. What was each son's share?

(b) Mrs. Sonal had written a will before her death saying that her property worth Rs. 87,65,92,600.00 should be shared between 13 charitable organisations. How much did each organisation get?

(c) On school Sports Day, 7440 children of one of the biggest schools in our town had to be split into 4 major teams. Then each team was further divided into 6 sub teams. How many children will be there in each of the major teams and in each of the sub teams?

(d) Proiti bought tickets for 'The Young Ones' cricket match for 18 of her friends on Saturday, paying Rs. 5490.00. 12 more wanted to come for the match. So she went again on Sunday to buy tickets for them, but this time she had to pay Rs. 4920.00 for 12 tickets. How much did each ticket cost for each of the groups? How much more did each one from the second group have to pay compared to the children in the first group?

(e) The Indian cricket team won the Emirates Trophy and got a prize money equal to Rs. 48,72,096.00 from the sponsors. They got an additional bonus of Rs. 24,00,000.00 from the Cricket Board in India. If the number of recipients is 16, what is the total amount received by each participant?

(f) A large property was sold by a grandparent for Rs. 7,83,39,000.00 and the money was distributed amongst his 14 grandchildren. How much did each grandchild inherit?

Maths Lab Activity 2

Money around the world

Materials required

Coins and notes of different denominations of a few countries

Method (Note for the Teacher)

Show the coins to the students in the class to find out if anyone knows the names of currency from another country. Discuss the colour, size and value of the coins.

Next, divide the students into groups and let each group choose a country. Each group should go to the library and read through the encyclopaedia to research about that country's money (coins, currencies, and their values). They should try to get a few coins, if possible, as samples from friends and relatives to show to others. The students can also be provided with clay to create some coins they see in books. In the process, they should also find out some information about the country. Each group should also find out how much will Rs. 100.00 be equal to in the currency of the chosen country. Once all the groups have collected enough information, they could present it to the entire class. A large world map can be put up in class for the students to identify the countries.